Place:
Canfield

By

Bob Gentzel

Publication Data

Book Title	Place: Canfield
Author	Bob Gentzel
Copyright	© 2015
Publisher	Bookbaby
ISBN	978-1-94361-286-4

Preface

This is a tale of growing up in Canfield, Ohio during the 1950's and 60's. While the story follows me, the tale isn't about me.

I wasn't special—just one more baby boomer kid. My memories, the thoughts and feelings of each day, my twists and turns through those years were ordinary--common to countless others of that generation.

Rather, the tale is about the place that surrounded, that pushed and pulled at kids like me, and the tugs within us that created the experience of growing in that time and place.

And along the way, within the daily commonplace, something remarkable took form.

Events in Canfield didn't unfold exactly as I've written--after fifty years, memory weakens. Moreover, I sometimes altered names or tweaked a detail to shield innocence, respect privacy or protect a memory another might share and hold dear. Beyond that, this is as close as I can recall.

Contents

I.	Landscape	5
II.	Fresh Contour	13
III.	Rising	17
IV.	Building Up, Tearing Down	34
V.	Stirrings	66
VI.	Dimensions	89
VII.	Echoes	131
VIII.	No Signposts	155
IX.	Clinging	178
X.	Perspective	190
XI.	Enduring Forms	202
XII.	Renewal	204

Each of us enters the world with his own landscape. And from our earliest days onward, we dwell in those lands.

Look into a child's eyes. The contours of that young landscape are veiled and hazy. No roads or passageways yet exist. In fragile first light, the lands stretch outward. But the ways are unknown and uncharted. In the dawning, vague contours and dim paths may begin to emerge.

Station

The railroad track came in from the north. It emerged from far woods and cut across stubble cornfield, carried along on a slight fill. Dried brush, a tangle of bushes and spent leaves lined its progression, dividing railroad from the expanse of the field. Veiled in the low brush, the single track reached southward, angling toward a grade crossing at Herbert Road. Weathered poles rose from the bushes at intervals along the line. The poles were strung with a few thin wires which drooped, and rose, then sagged again to the cadence of the poles.

As we neared the faded crossbuck, Mom slowed our '51 Dodge, and we bumped up onto the track. From the back seat I peered north. A low, gray sky dulled my view—no trains. The rails were worn, ties and joints pounded down, ballast uneven—light slag strewn on blackened cinders, heaped here and there. Ends of a few discarded crossties poked through dry weeds lining the track. Our rear tires thumped against the rails, and we cleared the crossing.

I quick turned and glanced the other direction—no trains there either. The railroad continued southward across another field of beige corn stubble and open earth, gradually curving away into a stand of darkened trees, a gentle rise in the woods, and out of sight. A mile beyond the bend the railroad would emerge again from the woods, cross US Route 224 and enter the town of Canfield.

Land

In 7th grade Ohio History we learned a glacier had pushed through town during the Ice Age. The sheet of ice had plowed down from Canada, flattening hills and filling the valleys like a giant road grader. It stopped at the terminal moraine somewhere in central Ohio. Our textbook maps told us Canfield was in that transition zone near the end of the glacier's span. So to the north, towards Lake Erie, the fields were straight and flat, while thirty miles to the south the hills of southern Ohio began to rise up.

The land around Canfield flowed in low hills and long, gentle ridges. Small streams and creeks wandered the base of the ridges, carrying moisture from the earth east toward the Mahoning and beyond into the Ohio. The land was smooth and contained. From the top of a ridge you might see out a couple miles across fields and farm, or over broad stretches of full woods and treetops to the next ridge, but that was as far as it went. There were no canyons or wide river valleys, no great vistas stretching to hazy horizons or high peaks looming in the distance. The far ridges hinted at something beyond, but never quite opened to it.

Scattered houses dotted the ridges and hills. The old houses, some going back to the early 1900's, were isolated—a quarter acre yard carved against the woods. A gravel driveway led to a square two-story house in need of fresh, white paint. The home sat sheltered behind a pair of Norway spruce trees planted in the front yard when the house was new, the trees now grown too big for the space. Out back, a row of socks, pillowcases and undershirts hung from the clothesline, airing in the breeze. Nearby, a small vegetable garden took in the sun. The good soil always produced a yard of strong green grass and more ripe tomatoes than you could keep up with.

Much of Canfield was farm country. Family farms and barns, open pastures and fields broke the woodlands. Corn, hay and dairy cattle predominated. Each open field was preceded by an ample farmhouse, a massive barn, several sheds, corn cribs and out buildings clustered nearby. Always a round silo rose up to vie with the treetops.

The barn of faded red paint was walled in rows of broad, vertical boards. Barn beams and timbers rested on a thick stone foundation and held firm under a slate roof--the gray tile pattern marked in dark tiles with the year of construction: 1910, 1896…. Pigeons kept watch from the slate roof line. A few rested along the eaves, near gaps in wall boards warped wide enough for the birds to enter and flap inside to musty nests high atop the beams. There within, the air was full with odors of hard corn, muddy hogs and aged hay bales.

From early spring to late fall, tractors rolled out from the barns and sheds, towing manure spreaders, plows, harrows and balers, to crisscross the fields. Tilled acres spread outwards and covered the land beside rural roads. On the backside of the plowed fields, away from the roads, tracts of thick woods at the last fences marked the edge of the property line.

Town

Canfield followed a simple order. At its heart was the village green, an open lawn a hundred feet wide, three blocks long. The green ran north/south, bordered on each side by Broad Street. Broad split at the north end of the green and rejoined at the south end. Main Street, Route 224, ran east/west, intersecting Broad at the two traffic lights in the center of town. Lisbon Street entered the green from the southwest, a block south of Main.

The green harbored a mix of stately American elms, silver maples, sugar maples and oaks. Their branches rose over the common space, over the bandstand and park benches, reaching outward above the parallel Broad Street pavements. In winter the green collected an accumulation of snows, its border edged in heaps of gritty, plowed snow and dreary slush kicked up by traffic along Broad. In summer, the green was mowed often and well-tended, offering cool shade to those who passed.

Along Broad Street, around the perimeter of the green, stood a dozen homes together with small shops, churches and businesses. The structures faced inward, a common focus upon the green. This assembly of buildings formed a core, drawing people of the township together. Each day they came. The daily comings and goings of the community to this place were unhurried. The pace was calm, but purposeful.

Shops and businesses occupied one and two-story brick buildings along the west side of the green, between Main and the south end of the square. McCabe Drug, with its offering of comic books in revolving metal racks, and the Neff Insurance Agency stood near the corner at Lisbon Street. Close by, Isaly's Dairy was a fixture. Half

7

gallon bottles of milk, squares of butter, slabs of Swiss cheese and quart boxes of Neapolitan ice cream filled coolers behind the glass counter. The lunch menu in the side booths listed grilled cheese, thin chopped ham and BLT's on Wonder Bread. Sandwiches were served with a few slices of dill pickle and a handful of chips. The turning barber shop pole hung next door—sometimes I'd walk there after school for a haircut. Next to the barber shop, the shelves at the Five and Ten were packed with a studied assortment of articles on sale for a handful of change. There were the merely practical, like writing paper, rulers and #2 pencils for school, along with the absolutely necessary, like kite string, pea shooters and caps for your six-gun.

On the corner of Broad and Main, next to the traffic light, was the one room A&P. Outside, tall display windows and a broad red and gold A&P sign stretched across the front—the building looked like an old time general store. Inside, Mom would walk up to the counter, hand the proprietor a list, and he'd begin fetching items, one by one, from shelves lining the high walls, pushing about a ladder on rollers to reach the highest articles. Next door, the Fountain dated from the 1930's. With high ceilings, classic long soda counters and round swivel stools, it still made the best milk shakes in town.

Anchoring the block was the Farmers National Bank building. The bank's imposing stone columns and gray chiseled façade stood a rung above other local businesses. People always quieted going inside the Bank, the same way they did entering church on Sunday.

Most homes on the green were north of Main--solid, two-story wooden construction, respectable, with plain Midwest lines and ample porches. Interspersed were several three-story homes, larger and ornate, dating to Victorian times. They lent a dignified air to that section of the green. The yellow Parkview House occupied the knoll at the north end, where Broad Street split. Years earlier, the Parkview had been converted from private residence to fine restaurant. The Parkview catered to the after-church crowd on Sunday afternoons. I aspired to dine at the Parkview on Sunday, but my family didn't go there—we were more of an Isaly's kind of clientele.

Gas stations occupied three corners at Main and Broad. Pumping gas for the steady flow of traffic along 224, fixing flats, changing oil and doing tune-ups and repairs for the locals proved enough to sustain the filling stations. A block away, the Pennzoil station at Broad and Lisbon also stayed busy. But the small red-tile roof Texaco station, tucked beside the library at the south end of the green, wasn't so fortunate. It sat empty and unused.

East of the green, across from Isaly's and the Five and Ten, were the Methodist Church and the Mahoning Dispatch. Housed in a tiny one story building, the Dispatch began producing a weekly newspaper in 1877. Some eighty years later its ancient printing press continued to chronicle news around Mahoning County at the personal level. Each Friday, across the low hills from Calla to West Austintown, from Washingtonville to Berlin Center, the Dispatch recounted surprise visits of aunts and cousins from Indiana, Helena Delf's call on Pittsburgh relatives, births of daughters, shipments of apples at fall harvest, the October marriage of Phil Wetmore to Daisy Smith, sons departing for the service, and 4-H winners at the county fair. Beside the Dispatch stood the tan brick and brown stone of the Methodist parsonage and Church. Each morning the church's tall bell tower and adjacent elms cast shade across the commons. And each evening, descending sunlight would angle across the village green, illuminate the Church's broad stained glass window of Jesus and his flock, and come to rest within the Methodist sanctuary. Together the little newspaper and neighboring church proclaimed the worth of area lives.

Next to the Dispatch, the gray painted Township Hall building was still. In earlier times it had housed local government work and occasional Friday night community dances. But by the 1950's, township offices had relocated to the second floor of the new brick fire station a couple blocks west on Lisbon Street.

South of the Methodist Church stood the Dairy Isle, and beside it, the Dairy Queen. To many Canfield grownups, the fast-food stands were eyesores, not worthy of a position on the green. Each was a small lean-to affair with flat, sloping roof. The Dairy Isle advertised a ten foot, red and green steel ice cream cone rising above roofline. Customers didn't enter these buildings, but walked to the front beneath the overhanging roof to place orders and collect burgers, shakes and custard cones through the sliding screen window. On summer days, hotdogs sputtered and steamed on turning stainless steel rollers inside the front window, as breezes carried the scent of warm hamburger grease across the commons.

Kids didn't share their parents' view of the custard businesses. By the late 50's the Dairy stands had replaced The Fountain as the local hangout. Out front, teenagers sipping Cokes milled about the sidewalks, while younger kids gathered on bicycles in the gravel parking lots behind. Why two competitors located next to each other never made sense. But like the gas stations on Main, they persisted.

The Normal School dominated the south end. An impressive, white stone and brick building—it was the largest structure on the commons. The building had served as Mahoning County courthouse in the mid 1800's before the county seat, with its complement of judges and lawyers, was wrestled away by Youngstown. The building became a teachers' school in the late 1800's, but education there ended in the early 1900's. By the 1950's law and professional offices occupied the building, and kids had little reason to go inside.

Across from the Normal School, next to the idle Texaco station, stood the two-story, red brick Public Library. The building dated to the depression, when the WPA laid the bricks and constructed the heavy, gray slate roof. Books were housed on the first floor, and occasional visitors researched a school project or hunted a favorite biography amid the stacks, subject always to the strict enforcement of quiet.

But every Thursday evening that stillness was broken. At 7 pm Boy Scout Troop 25 met in the basement of the library to practice marching and saluting, plan the next campout, sing Old Lady Leary and other favorites, and compete in knot tying and Morse code. After the meeting, scouts exited to the green to roughhouse at keep away, red rover and other noisy games. Gradually calm would return to the village as scouts who lived in the country began loading into parents' cars for the drive home, shouts diminished, the games wound down and scouts from town scattered to the sidewalks, some exiting the square as they rounded the corner by

10

the Pennzoil station, and a few others pausing for a Coke at the Dairy Isle on their walk home.

Beyond the green, modest homes and quiet neighborhoods radiated outward. To the north, along Callahan and Sleepy Hollow, houses were post-war suburban. Many of the nicer homes in town, new ranches and split levels, were here. South and east of the green, behind the Methodist Church and Dairy Isle, along Fairview and Hood Drive were a mix of suburban and modest small town homes. A little beyond Hood, the cemetery on Main Street and, to the south, the fairgrounds off Broad marked that edge of the village.

Southwest of the green, a row of impressive homes—a couple with big, white front porch columns--lined Court Street, near the old court house. A block behind them rose the village water tower, the highest point in town. The round, gray tank jutted above treetops. Like the crown of a distant ridge, it marked the village from afar. In the long shade of the water tower, an older section of the village spread along Lisbon Street as that road led southwest out of town. Here houses were 1920's vintage, small town wooden construction, respectable, modest and well cared for. Just off Lisbon, Edwards Avenue bordered the back of the schoolyard and high school football field. And a couple blocks beyond Edwards, at the outskirts of the village, the railroad track cleared the grade crossing at Route 224, entering the village as it drew towards the depot.

The track paused at Newton Street, beside the white painted, green trim Erie station. There thin wires swung from trackside poles to droop and meet the station, and the railroad broadened to a couple short sidings serving the local lumber yard, a small grain elevator and the loading dock along John Delf's & Sons feed supply barn. A spur poked across Lisbon Street opposite Delf's, parted the roadside weeds and butted up to a coal trestle. The concrete frame and steel bents of the trestle supported a black grit coal hopper unloaded earlier that day--many homes and businesses in town still burned bituminous. Finally, just beyond Lisbon Street, the sidings

11

merged, the railroad narrowed back to a single, lone track, and worn rails left the village, reaching again southward, returning to the countryside.

Canfield wasn't unusual. The village arose and worked and rested upon the same foundation as thousands of other small towns spread across Ohio and the Midwest. Growing up, I passed those traffic lights at Main and Broad countless times--so often and routinely that each passing should have been nothing more than unremarked habit.

But for some reason, it wasn't. For some reason I always felt a little special, a little privileged, to be there ... to cross the green each morning on the school bus ride along Main, to glance northward to the Parkview on afternoon rides home, to explore the isles of the Five and Ten at springtime in search of a new balsa wood kite, or to sit in a booth at Isaly's enjoying a slice of dill pickle. Maybe I sensed a little then what we later come to realize—that the place we live is, in fact, special. And each day that place infuses, fills and forms us, and we meld with it in ways we'll probably never quite understand.

II.

The young landscape emerges in fresh contour, and the forms of that land catch the feel of our days. Our surface moves--each day the contours are in play, sculpted and shaped by sensations that find and move us. And as we are first shaped, as our early forms shift and emerge, we come to color the expanse around us and beyond our reach with shades and hues already within our span.

First Light

My family lived in the country on Palmyra Road, about four miles west of the village. Ours was one of six houses huddled together as you came down off the gentle ridge at the corner of Palmyra and Turner Road. Guernsey cows grazed in a pasture behind the neighbor's back yard. Across the road an old farmer and his wife tended a vegetable patch each summer and worked their field of a couple acres. On sunny days the old man chugged up and down the corn rows on a spindly red Harvester tractor. My older sister Carol had a classmate two houses away, but no boys lived nearby. Aside from the milkman in the morning, the afternoon mailman and the school bus twice a day, traffic up and down Palmyra was sparse. Beyond our little outpost, we were surrounded by woods.

Our yard provided ample play space. Along the side yard, Carol, my younger sister Nancy and I found a little opening within small trees and bushes and called it the "hideout," inspired by the Lone Ranger on Saturday mornings. Beyond the back yard, under a row of trees bordering the Guernsey pasture was our "swimming pool," a muddy depression several feet across that filled with a few inches of water when it rained. In the back corner of the yard, a scraggly willow with short branches became our Peter Pan "Pirate Ship." Mom kept an eye on the three of us as we ran around the yard, in and out of the trees, chasing bad guys, climbing to the crow's-nest and riding to the rescue.

In time, Carol, Nancy and I wandered deeper into the woods behind our house. We found the "coal mine," a half acre plot scattered with brambles and undulating heaps of coal and shale. The digging had ended there long ago, and blackberry bushes were taking over the heaps. Out past the swimming pool I built a tiny

13

shelter one day with bundles of dried, beige weeds tied together. It was just big enough to crawl inside, and I was proud to show it off to Dad when he came home from work that day. I learned how to climb elms near the swimming pool to get a good view of Mom's garden, and once I pushed into the woods and discovered a little stream and small waterfall churning away under the trees, its sharp whoosh of water cutting into a pool below.

And there was the day I ventured beyond where our family had picked blackberries a week earlier and chanced upon a broad, massive tree, its smooth trunk several feet wide. Its branches sheltered a soft, open area enclosing the trunk—a clearing seemingly set apart from the rest of the forest. A covering of May apples—umbrella plants we called them—sprouted low in the shade. It looked like some forest spirit, mysterious but friendly, should live in the calm clearing under the tree.

And with each new pathway, each exploration and discovery, a tiny bit of the landscape became populated with the simple nature of things.

Beyond

Whenever I heard a train whistle, my ears perked up. A shiver ran through me, and I had to look for that train. It was always like that—I was attuned to trains.

First there were train pictures in our stack of Little Golden Books at home. In one story Donald Duck circled his yard riding a miniature railroad train, stopping each round by the station and water tank. In another story, Scuffy the Tugboat sailed down streams and rivers to a great ocean port, where docks teemed with railroad boxcars filled with goods to be loaded aboard ships. In another book, a boy journeyed cross country on a glistening streamliner, leaving behind a maze of tracks in the big city as the train sped toward the mountains. I couldn't read the words, but I understood the pictures.

Dad set up the Lionel train under the tree at Christmas. He built a mountain tunnel of plaster and a railroad suspension bridge for the train, and the smoke from the black locomotive puffed around the circle, past the station with a green roof, across the wire bridge, and rose into the tree branches and bright ornaments encircling the tunnel. The big wheels on the locomotive turned in unison, like the ones at the beginning of Superman on TV, when the announcer said "More powerful than a speeding locomotive…."

Encounters with real trains were by chance. When a package once came to the station in Canfield, Mom put on her navy blue wool coat, loaded up Carol, Nancy and me in the back seat of the Dodge and drove to town. Big wooden steps by the track led up to the station platform and the doorway inside. The station man took a couple minutes to fetch Mom's package, but no trains happened by when we were inside. When we returned to our parked car, I didn't want to leave—I wanted to stay to see if a train would come.

Sometimes Mom drove us to Leetonia to stock up on Dan Dee potato chips. At the potato chip factory she bought a tin of chips so big it lasted for weeks. The smell of hot chip oil hung over town and scented the railroad tracks near the factory. On one visit, a powerful freight train appeared, pounding around the curve and blowing his whistle. The noise of the train and its long string of boxcars filled the town, pushing aside even the potato chip smell.

Occasional drives to Youngstown offered the best chance to see real trains. Steel mills throughout the Mahoning Valley were laced with railroad tracks. Smoky freight yards of coal and ore fed the furnaces. Tracks along the massive buildings moved with hoppers of slag, hot metal trains, sooty switch engines shuffling gondolas of steel slabs, and a busy array of passing boxcars. As I learned to read, I came to recognize the names on the trains: B&O, New York Central, Erie…. In time I learned to connect the names to the lines across the maps in Mom's Hammond's <u>Atlas of the United States</u>. And each Christmas a new Lionel catalogue presented images of more trains and new railroad names: Union Pacific, Great Northern, Rock Island …

The trains reached out to a land beyond.

There wasn't much you could do about it. Like going to the dentist, church was something you just had to put up with. On Saturday night if Mom announced, "We're going to church tomorrow morning," you could moan all you wanted. But you were going—Ivory Soap clean, all shined up in good pants, white shirt and bow tie, hair plastered stiff with Wave Set.

We were new to Canfield, and Mom and Dad were looking for a church they liked, where the family might fit in. We tried the Presbyterian Church on Main Street, a couple blocks west of the green. It was an old building, laid with large, blackened, rectangular stones. On Sunday mornings you climbed a heavy stone stairway to enter the front door. Mom and Dad would lead Carol, Nancy and me inside and deposit us in the Sunday school rooms in the basement. Then they'd leave us behind, returning upstairs to attend the service. Nothing fun ever happened in Sunday school—teachers told stories and you had to behave. Being in Sunday school was like having a baby sitter.

Sunday school teachers had lots of stories--Bible stories of people with unusual names who lived a long time ago on the other side of the world. Some stories made sense, but there were plenty you weren't too sure about. How exactly could a person get two of every kind of bird and animal loaded onto an arc? Did the sea really open just because Moses wanted it to? And what about those shepherds at Christmas—did they really see angels who told them about Jesus? In fairy tales like Peter Pan and Snow White you knew the magic was make believe. But in Bible stories God was supposed to be in the background, behind the scenes, making impossible things really happen. Things like that didn't happen in Canfield—no one I knew had ever spotted an angel. So you had to wonder.

Of course, once every year real magic came to town—Christmas. In Sunday school we heard the stories of Jesus in the manger and learned to sing "Joy to the World." That set the stage for the honest-to-goodness magic each December. Santa Claus wasn't in the Bible, but his visit on Christmas Eve and those presents under the tree Christmas morning were proof enough that reindeer could fly and gifts brought joy. For us Sunday school kids, Santa Claus did more for church than all those Bible stories put together.

III.

Down low, far under our earth, a force struggles ... a molten force that first compelled our forms to rise. It heaves upward, lifting the mass of our landscape, the stuff of our being. In its rising, the land assumes breadth. Pebbles of childhood days may fuse, causing a swell to increase, a spring to well up and a breeze to billow forth in cloud. Modest hills poke and press forth, and we seek a path about them.

School

School was an overarching exercise, a work that grounded the days and unified the years. Each numbered grade marked a step in the annual progression. Around each step, daily life revolved.

I disliked school. As the years rolled on, dislike grew to hate. School was a cruel, compulsory sentence. Each day it forced you forward, a step beyond your comfort zone, luring with the hope of affirmation and success, and threatening with a mark of failure. Always another direction to follow, section to read, assignment to learn, question to answer and expectation to confront. It smothered life.

But, too, school offered comfort and strength. The directed course from kindergarten through 12th guided through any undercurrents and helped push you along. With each grade, each rung, you understood where you had been, knew where you were in the order of things and could anticipate what was coming next. The system churned with assembly line predictability. Each year older kids confronted their new level and then advanced--a hopeful example for the younger who would next replace them.

And there was strength in numbers. Together with classmates you pressed on, fighting the same pressures, building toward an uncertain but common goal, drawing strength from one another and finding shelter in the herd. Most everybody made it through.

Kindergarten

Mom drove me to school the first day of kindergarten. She had done the same with Carol two years before. Now it was my turn. Mom steered onto Wadsworth, parked in the big gravel lot opposite the schoolyard, and led me across the street to school. We entered the building together through heavy doors at the main front entrance and turned left into the kindergarten room. She spoke a few minutes with two older, lady teachers, as I looked around the room at the long tables with tiny wooden chairs and the row of metal coat hooks on the dark wooden board along the back wall. I watched a group of kids playing on the floor with big rectangular, smooth-sanded wooden blocks. It seemed some of the kids knew each other, but I didn't know any of them. When Mom finished talking, she turned back to me to make sure I was OK, and then she left. I was uneasy. This wasn't like playing in the backyard at Palmyra Road. I could see things were going to be different.

The public school was a short walk west of the green. The oldest part of the building housed the brown brick grade school, old auditorium and gym. It dated to 1922. Carol's classroom was somewhere inside. My kindergarten room was in front, looking out on Wadsworth. The adjoining junior high and high school sections were newer tan brick, off to the right of the grade school. The school was the largest building in town—each day hundreds of kids from across the township assembled there. And so on that September day, along with Roger and Linda, Kathleen, Diane and Donna, Mark and Bonnie and Carl and Bobby A. and Bobby H., with Bill and Richy and Jimmy and Billy and Larry, with Tommy, Walter, Janice, Kathy and all the others, Bobby G. joined the Canfield kindergarten herd.

Apart from those first couple minutes of kindergarten, I remember only a few things from that year …   In the beginning it was important not to lose the little piece of paper Mom had pinned to my shirt that said "Bus Number 4." I wanted to play wooden blocks with Bonnie and Carl, but the two of them weren't interested in my joining in. Sometimes the class sat in the tiny chairs at the long tables and took tests where the teacher told you to draw a yellow ring with a green diamond on it. Even when you wore your smock—which was really just one of your Dad's old shirts you put on backwards--finger painting was messy. The classroom contained a glass jar a foot tall with a metal lid. The jar was filled with white paste for gluing paper. The paste smelled bad and didn't hold paper together very well. In the afternoon Nancy would wait next to the mailbox at the end of our driveway on Palmyra Road for Bus 4 to stop and let off Carol and me. Nancy missed us. Next year would be her turn.

First Grade

Kindergarten was a prelude to the real thing. With first grade, the rhythm began in earnest. Up early, get dressed, eat breakfast, out to catch the bus, a long morning at school, slow afternoons watching the clock, and finally returning home on the bus late afternoon.

Mrs. Lowry's first grade was in the row of classrooms at the back of the school, on the ground floor behind the auditorium and old gym. You entered her classroom from a dark hallway with high ceilings. The room was ringed on three sides with blackboards and easels, shelves and coat hooks, with the American flag pinned high to the wall near the PA speaker up front. Her desk was below the flag. Tall windows filled the side wall. Their glass panes began about waist high and stretched upward to the ceiling. Big cast iron radiators protruded from the wall below the windows. Outside was the playground.

Every day started with the Pledge of Allegiance followed by morning announcements over the PA. Then the day's activities began. In that room we first graders practiced show and tell, learned to listen, add, read, wait for your turn, write the alphabet and behave.

School was for learning, but my heart was in recess. A couple times a day we put on our jackets and Mrs. Lowry led the class down the dark hall to the side door. We exited, turned right and walked a few steps to the gate which opened to the playground behind the school.

The playground was big, bordered along the front by the grade school building, on one side by high school locker rooms and on the back by the high school football field (that was off limits). A tall chain link fence under a row of maples marked the last side. During recess, teachers usually sat on a couple of benches under the maples.

The playground was a grayish area—there were scattered patches of grass, but most of the ground was covered with hard, gray pea

19

gravel. In heavy traffic lanes, like the bottom of the sliding board, the gravel had been pounded down into the hard dirt. In more sheltered areas, like near the teachers' benches, the gravel had been kicked up into little, loose piles a couple inches deep. You had to be careful running where there were piles, because the gravel would slip around and you could fall.

Playground equipment was worn gray steel, tinged here and there with dark rust. Closest to the school was a row of teeter totters-- long wooden planks balanced on a steel fulcrum. Even in first grade, kids knew that when you were down and your teeter buddy was up, you could suddenly jump off, sending your buddy teetering down to a hard whack on his rear when his end hit the ground. Nobody played on the teeter totters very much. Nearby was the merry-go-round, an eight-foot flat steel circle with short railings radiating from the center. To make it spin, you pushed the end of the railing, running alongside in a circle, and then you'd hop on for the ride. When the platform was going really fast you had to hold on to the railing to keep from getting spun off. The pushing track encircling the merry-go-round was worn down--it became a puddle when it rained.

The metal sliding board was well polished with a daily buffing of jeans and dungarees. The monkey bars in the middle of the playground rose seven or eight feet at their center. The bars were popular—even their darkened rusty spots were smooth from constant use. Farthest from the school, near the edge of the football field, were two big metal swing sets. Instead of dangling ropes or chains, steel rods supported the seats, each rod about a half inch in diameter and ten inches long. The rods were looped together at their ends, forming a kind of extended chain. Rhythmic squeaking of the metal loops signaled when the swings were in use.

During recess, small bands of first grade boys roamed the playground, chasing each other and trying to catch the leader of the rival band. Jimmy led his band of several guys and I led another. One day in the middle of the chase I headed for the merry-go-round. It had rained the day before, and the pushing track was full of water. I leaned forward over the muddy puddle, grabbed one of the railings and gave a good shove to keep the merry-go-round turning before I hopped on. After a few times around, I jumped off, but I slipped and fell backward, splashing into the water. I twisted around and stood up. The whole backside of my jeans was soaked, and all the kids were looking at me. I stood there a moment, wondering what to do. Then Jimmy walked over to me. "You need to go tell the teacher," Jimmy said. That made sense. She would know what to do. So he and I walked over to Mrs. Lowry who was sitting on the benches, talking with other teachers. "Bobby fell in the water," Jimmy announced to the teacher.

Mrs. Lowry looked me over. "Turn around," she said. She seemed irritated. "Well, why don't you go back inside the classroom and sit down on the radiator."

I wasn't expecting that. Her instruction made sense, but I was expecting something better—like a dry pair of jeans she had tucked away in a drawer somewhere for emergencies like this. I had just embarrassed myself in front of the whole school—that was bad enough. And now Mrs. Lowry wanted me to go sit on the radiator, right inside the window--in full view of everybody still out on the playground. I felt like I was being punished when I hadn't done anything wrong. But she was the teacher.

The radiator was uncomfortable. Dirty water dripped down my legs as my rear heated up. Outside I watched classmates peering in at me, pointing and giggling. As I sat on the hot metal ridges of the radiator, the rhythmic squeak of the swings marked the minutes. Outside, roving bands continued the chase without me. At one point Jimmy came running up to the window with a big smile. "None of your men can seem to catch me," he yelled through the panes. He grinned again then turned and ran away.

I didn't appreciate Jimmy's teasing, because I knew if I was out there, I could catch him. Sure as shooting—I could catch him. And he knew it, too. But all I could do was sit there on display, helpless, like one of those hot dogs slow steaming on the rollers inside the window at the Dairy Isle.

Girls

You could see there were different kinds of birds. A blue jay wasn't the same as a sparrow, crows and cardinals were different, and ducks and robins didn't act the same. Like different birds, from early on I came to see the world was full of different kinds of girls.

21

First there were moms—that was the main group, the group you could count on. That was the group in charge.

Teachers formed the next group. They were like moms—a kind of mom away from home. But teachers didn't care about you as much as real moms, and teachers always had lots of orders and things for you to do.

Grandmas and older ladies like you saw in church generally left you alone. They weren't very interested in what you were doing and didn't expect nearly as much from you as moms and teachers expected.

And then there were girls, a whole school full of them. I didn't know what they expected, so I naturally kept a safe distance.

All the girl and lady groups seemed to share something unspoken, like they were all on the same side in a game of red rover. When a mom spoke with a teacher, it seemed they had a special understanding between them—they knew something together. When Kathy invited me to her birthday party, I was surprised how pleased Mom was about the invitation. I wasn't especially interested in the party, but the invitation seemed special for Mom, as if Mom and my little classmate shared some secret, and I was left on the outside looking in. The sharing seemed mysterious.

Happily, there was one more kind of girl, a special group—sisters. Sisters weren't mixed up in the mystery. Every morning Carol, Nancy and I ate our bowls of Rice Krispies, Cheerios or Kellogg's Sugar Pops, Mom poured each of us a glass of Welch's Grape Juice, and then we'd we set out on our Lone Ranger chases around the yard, or pile into the back seat of the car for the drive to town, or strike up an argument over the next comic book purchase at McCabe's Drug Store. Carol and Nancy were just Carol and Nancy. They weren't like other girls. Each of us always called the other two "you guys"--nothing mysterious about that. Like Welch's grapes, sisters were just part of the same bunch.

The elementary school playground was the site of many a pitched battle. Once or twice each recess a call would ring out over the schoolyard--"The merry-go-round! To the merry-go-round!" It didn't matter what you were doing when the shout was heard--in the middle of a big chase, standing out by the swings, or surveying the schoolyard from the top rung on the monkey bars—none of that mattered. When the call rang out, you were duty-bound to drop everything and come running.

From the earliest days of recess, everybody knew that boys pushed the merry-go-round so it turned counter-clockwise. Girls wanted to make it spin clockwise. So each recess when we passed through the playground gate, boys would make a bee line to the merry-go-round to get it spinning the right way. Once we got it going and the momentum was carrying it along, most of the boys would then jump off to play. A boy or two normally stayed on board to maintain the spin and guard against any effort by the girls to take over. It was all right if girls wanted to ride along—that was fine. We just didn't want them to reverse the spin.

Girls could be pretty coy about the merry-go-round battle. Most of the time, they acted as though they didn't care. Occasionally a couple of them would grab one of the push bars, dig their saddle shoes against the ground and try to slow down the turning. But the boys stationed on board would jump to action--their push was usually enough to keep the big steel platform spinning the right direction. Rather, it was the girls' big sneak attacks that were cause for alarm.

Sometimes a number of girls would casually make their way onto the merry-go-round, one by one over a period of time, quietly riding along, seemingly content turning the boys' way. Then suddenly, without warning, the band would spring, overwhelming the meager boy force left to protect the spin. The gang of Bonnie's and Kathy's and Beverly's and Barbara's would grab the pushing bars, pulling against the momentum, skidding their shoes against the dirt and pea gravel, trying to bring the merry-go-round to a stop. That's the moment when the cry would ring out from the boy guard—"To the merry-go-round!" And that's when Jimmy and Larry and Bobby and Richy and I and all the rest of the boys came running.

It was chaos when we arrived. The merry-go-round was stopped or barely turning—sometimes the girls had even reversed it. Amid the yelling and shouting boys and girls were pulling and pushing the steel frame opposite directions, competing for a good hand hold on the push bars, pigtails and pony tails bouncing, resisting the momentum, trying to force things their way. But once our boy reinforcements arrived, the battle never lasted long. After a few moments the grips on the soles of our Converse tennis shoes and Red Ball Jets, the heels of our cowboy boots began to dig in to that worn path around the merry-go-round, and the momentum shifted back counterclockwise. Slowly at first, then accelerating, we boys ran and pushed around the circle. After a few good turns, the girls accepted defeat, let go of the push bars, and Peggy and Mary and Bonnie and the others turned and skipped away, releasing the merry-go-round until the next battle.

After the contest we boys remained on board, turning merrily counterclockwise, happy knowing the natural order had been restored. For underneath the pushing and shoving, underneath the jockeying for position, underneath the coy strategies and scuffed saddle shoes, the reality was clear.

There was a girls' way, and there was a boys' way. Those ways spun in opposite directions. Boys and girls might somehow circle a common pathway, but our orbits were at odds. That elementary fact had emerged plain as day.

And so each recess, as Mrs. Lowry unleashed the class once again to the playground, boys and girls could expect the daily tugging and straining against one another to continue.

Second Grade

A week before second grade started, the school posted class lists in the hall outside the principal's office. The lists announced your teacher, your classroom and the names of classmates for the coming year. A lot of thought probably went into compiling those lists. But to a second grader, the orderly columns of clean, type-written names just appeared on the wall on the appointed day—a revelation from on high.

Checking lists was an anxious ritual, for the lists foretold much about the coming year. Was your new teacher good or bad, was she liked or feared? Where was your classroom? Were your friends in your class, or were they assigned to another? If chance smiled on you, a reading of the lists could leave you hopeful. For others, the lists might stir worry or fear.

Of course no sheet of paper could reveal all a new year might bring. But the lists were powerful. In the ordering of classes, the broad forms of the coming year began to take shape. The voice that would direct you the next nine months now became known. You understood who you would sit beside--the person whose last name started with the same letter as your name. New friends would emerge from those names who shared your room, while the unfamiliar names assigned to other classrooms--the names you never noticed as you scanned down the lists searching for your name--would remain strangers. The lists were like slowly swirling tea leaves rising to the surface.

Mrs. Carosella's second grade classroom was midway into the elementary school, halfway between the kindergarten room and the first grade classes, just off the old auditorium. The windows along one side of the room looked out to the front of the schoolyard, directly into the bus circle.

Mrs. Carosella was a large woman, a kind and caring teacher. Carol had Mrs. Carosella two years before. Since Carol was a good student, I think that helped Mrs. Carosella like me. I did well enough in class that year and my report cards were OK. But I was slow and had trouble with number facts. It always seemed to take me longer than other kids to complete written assignments and exercises. I worried that my brain didn't work as fast as others, but I felt it was important to get things right, so I didn't rush.

During the morning I looked forward to lunch. About 11 am the janitor began setting up collapsible lunch tables and benches in the auditorium. From our side of the closed classroom door, we listened to him banging and clanking away at the folding benches. At lunch time, if you bought your lunch, you went to the cafeteria, passed through the line to get your food, and ate in the old gym. If you brought your lunch from home, you ate at the collapsible tables in the auditorium. I always carried lunch from home in my Lone Ranger lunch box.

My lunch routine was always the same. Before sitting down with my friends Bobby and Buster and Billy, I went into the old gym and bought a half pint of white milk in a cardboard carton for three cents—you could buy chocolate milk for the same price. Then I returned to the auditorium with my milk and a paper straw. Sometimes Mom packed peanut butter and jelly, but usually it was a ham sandwich with mustard on Wonder Bread, all wrapped in wax paper, an orange cut into quarters and a Hostess Cream Filled Cupcake. I could count on it.

Mom regularly asked me if I wanted something different in my lunch for a change. But I didn't. I liked it the same every day.

The bus circle was the kids' version of the village green. Every morning, kids from all over the township came together in the bus circle. And every afternoon we boarded the big yellow buses parked around the circle to return home.

The bus driveway entered the front of the school from Wadsworth Street. It passed beneath a couple large elms and extended a hundred feet into the middle of the schoolyard. There it looped around in a big circle in front of the high school main entrance, and then exited on a parallel driveway a hundred feet back out to Wadsworth. Stubborn grass bordered the blacktop driveways and grew within the paved circle. An old black school bell rested on a brick pedestal in the center of the circle. The bell and faded bricks were all that remained of an earlier school building on that site, demolished a few years before to make room for more classrooms. From my seat in Mrs. Carosella's class, I enjoyed watching the afternoon buses pull in and line up around the circle. For when the buses began arriving, the school day was almost over.

The bus drivers liked to get there a little early. They'd pull into the driveway, counterclockwise around the circle as far as they could go, and park their buses single file. The whole fleet of about ten buses fit, looped around the driveway. On warm afternoons some of the drivers parked, then stepped off their buses to gather and talk somewhere on the circle, awaiting the dismissal bell. Most were older men, clean-shaven in denim coveralls or gray work clothes. Many wore old felt hats. Some of them, like Mr. Rogers on Bus 4, were local farmers who interrupted their field work twice a day for a little extra income.

When Mrs. Carosella dismissed class, you had only a few minutes to get things from your desk, collect your jacket from the wall hook, and go outside to find your bus. The circle was a beehive of kids swarming the buses in search of the right one, while other students from the village passed among the buses, beginning their walk home. Each driver's afternoon routine brought him to the circle about the same time every day, so your bus was usually about the same spot in the lineup. But if at first check it wasn't there, there was no time to dilly-dally. Then the best approach was to run to the first bus in the lineup and work your way back. The drivers were careful, and they tried to give kids enough time to get aboard. But once a driver closed the door, started the motor, and the lineup began to leave, it was hard for him to hear you pounding on the side of the moving bus, trying to get him to stop and reopen the door.

A long list of unwritten rules traveled aboard the buses. After an initial shake out period at the beginning of each school year, people usually sat in about the same seat every day, so you learned not to sit where you weren't welcome. If a girl sat down next to you, you could expect to be teased. The bus windows had big metal latches that you could release to pull down the window, but the window opened only half way. In first grade I learned that my head was small enough so that if I turned it sideways just right I could squeeze it through the window opening and poke my whole head outside into the wind. Then I learned that Mr. Rogers yelled at you when you did that and made you keep your head inside. The seats boys prized most were the two rear ones, up against the back of the bus. I tried to ride there whenever I could, until the day a truck bumped into the back of the bus when we were stopped on route 224. No one was hurt and the bus had only a little dent, but after that Mom told me not to sit back there anymore.

They didn't give you a report card for Bus Riding, but they should have.

Next to summer vacation, the best thing about school was Christmas. In mid-December they put up a real Christmas tree at the back of the old gym. The tree was huge—fifteen feet across and so tall it almost touched the ceiling. When it went up, writing exercises and reading groups wound down, and the hard school routine softened. Every grade school classroom spent hours making Christmas tree ornaments and decorations with colored paper, pipe cleaners, cotton, tin foil and glitter. This was the special occasion when you finally got a chance to use those unusual colors squeezed to the back of your Crayola box—the crayons not yet broken from overuse, the ones with strange names like Magenta and Burnt Sienna. As Christmas approached, every kid's little pair of shiny steel scissors with rounded points worked overtime. And the binding power of those smelly jars of white paste was tested in the competition that sprang up among classrooms to make the longest red and green paper chain.

The janitors decorated the tree the week before Christmas break. To reach the highest branches near the ceiling, they used wooden extension ladders shaped like an upside-down Y.

The finished tree was magnificent, covered in reindeer and wreaths, Santa's and snowflakes, paper candles, snowmen and angels, and draped from top to bottom with string after string of red and green paper chains. We all peered up and down the branches trying to find our special contribution.

On the last day of school before Christmas vacation, the whole grade school assembled in the gym. We sat on the wooden floor, spread around the tree, and sang Christmas carols. Teachers and principals, janitors and cafeteria ladies joined the gathering. From Frosty the Snowman to Silent Night, we sang them all. It was a special happy time, and everyone felt a part of it.

Valentine's Day was more complicated. First there was the box. A week before Valentine's everybody brought a cardboard box from home—you needed something at least the size of a shoe box. In

28

the box, you also brought the materials you would need to decorate. Then every day for a week Mrs. Carosella set aside time for us to work on our boxes. By the second or third day, the boxes began to take shape. By the end of the week, the works were complete.

There were boxes with sides covered in red paper with tiny white hearts, and tops covered with white paper and big red hearts with arrows. Some boxes were covered in shiny tin foil, with strips of red paper along the edges and the slot on top. Some kids edged their boxes with fancy white paper doilies from the Five and Ten, or decorated them with fuzzy red and white pipe cleaners bent in the shape of a heart. Each design had to allow for opening the box from the bottom or lifting off the lid to gather the cards inside. Mrs. Carosella had us write our name somewhere on our box, but names weren't necessary. By the end of the week everyone recognized each classmate's box.

Next came the task of choosing cards. I didn't want the mushy kind. So Mom helped me pick out ones with a picture of a fireman or cowboy that said something like "I'm aiming for you, Valentine." That was about as good a message as you could find. The cards came in a little pack. They were one-sided, with the picture on the front and the back blank with plenty of space for your name. At home the evening before Valentine's Day, I signed the back of each card with my first and last name, and then put the Valentines in a paper bag to take to school the next morning.

The hardest part of Valentine's Day was deciding who should get a card. When it was time for the exchange, each kid took his handful of cards and went around the room finding the right boxes and stuffing a card down the slot, like ballots in a ballot box. Determining which guys would get a card was easy—I knew my friends. Distributing cards to Bruce, Billy, Bobby and Mark was no problem. But deciding which girls would get a card was harder. Mom encouraged me to give a card to everyone in class, so no one would have hurt feelings. But all the fuss over Valentine's Day told me there was more to giving a card than just being polite. I didn't want to give a card out to just any girl. Trying to figure out what to do with the Valentine boxes belonging to the likes of Barbara, Jane,

Beverly, Bonnie and Jackie was a big problem. I never quite knew what to do.

When the cards were all stuffed away into the boxes, we sat back down at our desks, and it was time for food. Every classroom had a room mother, a classmate's mom who came to school to help out during parties and special times. Our room mother helped Mrs. Carosella pour juice and pass out cupcakes and little powdered sugar hearts with Valentine messages. Everyone got equal portions. We ate, opened our Valentine boxes and looked on the back of the cards to see who had sent a Valentine. I would never admit it, but as I shuffled through the cards I looked for some girls' names more than others.

Woods

About second grade my family moved from Palmyra Road to Pleasant Valley Lane. Pleasant Valley was on the other side of town, about four miles northeast of Canfield. More houses populated the area than I was used to on Palmyra. But beyond the houses, there was an abundance of new woods to explore and clear creeks to follow.

The woods along Pleasant Valley became my new stomping ground. Its paths connected the special places. The main path entered along the creek near our house. Trees there were low-- about fifteen feet--as young growth was reclaiming a field of a decade before. The path snaked through the low trees, following the water downstream. Here, the creek was narrow and shallow-- six feet wide and only a foot or two at its deepest. But it flowed year round, even on dry, hot summer days.

On a July day, the creek was alive with glistening green and blue dragon flies patrolling its course, water skippers flitting over the surface, and frogs jumping into pools when your approach disturbed their sunning. The water bubbled along over mossy stones, minnows darting about, and crayfish scuttling between the smooth rocks resting at the bottom. After a short stretch along the creek, the path turned to cross the water at the big beech tree. Here the stream opened and slowed to a quiet pool ten feet across. Several big rocks twisted the water at the entrance to the pool, and you could hop from rock to rock, across the stream to the shelter of

30

the tree. The beech rose from the edge of the water, its roots holding the bank firm, its massive trunk reaching up and gray branches spreading outward into the sky. Green papery leaves and light gray bark protected the quiet water. The calm of that spot always invited you to pause.

Beyond the beech, the path divided. One footpath cut away from the creek, through gnarled crab apple trees, past a couple of anthills and then rejoined the water downstream. In this stretch the stream was much wider. It flowed in from the right around a gentle bend, past short maples, oaks and bushy willows at the water's edge, and turned again as it cut into a muddy bank several feet high. Clumps of grass and weeds held the top of the bank together, and the path proceeded along the grassy edge. Another beech, this one smaller than the first, grew sideways a few feet out of the bank before the trunk then bent upward, lifting a tall tree over the water. Its leaves and branches hid a secret spot on the trunk where you could take your pocket knife and carve the initials of your girlfriend. The path continued downstream until it met a wire fence and stopped at the edge of a wide, sloping pasture. The people who owned the pasture land could look out the back windows of their house and see you walking the field, so I usually turned around at the fence.

The other footpath followed the creek away from the beech pond, through a low, muddy area of weeds and willows sprouting along the twisty waterway. A second creek flowed into the main creek amid the willows, forming a wider stream. There was no good way through there, so the path broke up in the lowlands. Sometimes you could get through by walking over the weeds and soggy ground, while times of high water forced you to hop and balance along, atop willow roots and low trunks. The path reformed on the opposite side of the creek, heading away from the water and upward into a hill of tall trees.

Part of the fun of the woods was running paths, dodging right and left around tree trunks, past thickets, and under low branches. Even better was the challenge of running the woods where there were no paths, to spring forward through the undergrowth, around the trees, avoiding brambles, ducking grapevines, hopping over branches fallen to the forest floor. This stretch amid tall trees was made for that kind of running. Once my friend Larry was visiting

31

and we ran the tall trees. Larry was from town--the neighborhood behind the Dairy Isle. So he didn't have much experience running the woods. He struggled to keep up through the tall trees and later told me I ran like a deer—in kid circles, that was a real compliment.

Beyond the hillside of tall trees, the footpath came to an end at the hollow oak tree--this was the payoff. The big oak trunk stood almost four feet wide and thirty feet tall. The tree looked dead, but a few stubborn branches sprouted near the top of the trunk, pushing forth a batch of leaves each summer. Many years before, someone had cut an opening waist high into the base of the trunk. You could squeeze through that opening and into the hollow. Inside there was plenty of room for two or three kids. But the most remarkable thing about this tree was that someone had nailed short boards, about fourteen inches long, to the inside of the hollow, forming a ladder, so you could climb way up inside the trunk.

The wooden steps and insides of the old hollow were covered in moist, dark red powder of rotting wood. Spider webs were everywhere, and the dank powder sprinkled down on you whenever you shook the tree, even just a little. Halfway up, the wooden steps seemed ready to give way, and I hated spiders. But the lure of climbing up to the top step and peering out into the woods through the rotting trunk made the climb mandatory for any self-respecting kid.

I used the woods as I pleased. I didn't know or care if it belonged to anyone—as far as I was concerned it was mine. Sometimes I'd stomp aside grasses, milkweeds and cattails and blaze a new path, or chop down a small tree to lay a foot bridge of a couple logs over the creek, or take a shovelful of one ant hill and dump it on another to watch the battle. But my marks didn't last--each year the weeds and ants and trees re-grew, and my playground was preserved.

About age ten, I got a Daisy BB pump rifle. It was a perfect marriage. Could there be a better feeling than coming home from the store with a bag full of cardboard cylinders full of shiny new BB's, happy in the knowledge you had enough ammo to last for weeks?

BB guns were made for roaming the woods. Trees, rocks and fence posts made good targets. A leaf or stick floating downstream just dared you to aim and shoot. Shooting insects was fun—I was known to have brought down dragonflies in mid air. Hunting frogs around the edge of the water was good sport—if you hit the frog's spine on the back of his head, right between his eyes the second he sprang, he would die instantly with his legs and forearms frozen in an extended jump position. A BB wouldn't kill them, but snakes always deserved a shot, especially any snake hanging around the water. And so bugs and frogs and reptiles were fair game.

But a boundary formed at chipmunks, birds and squirrels. In my early BB gun days I sometimes shot at them. But the excitement of trying to hit a moving squirrel or watching a puff of feathers topple from a tree never measured up to the regret of bloody feathers and a struggling animal lying in front of me on the ground. Fur and feathers became off limits.

So my woods persisted from year to year, and I took for granted it would always be there. But every so often, at the edge of a pasture or a grouping of trees, wooden stakes would unexpectedly appear, pounded into the ground to mark the corners of another foundation. Soon trees would come down, concrete footers would be poured, cement blocks would be set, 2X4's would go up and another house arose, marring my fields and stealing my woodland. Each discovery of new stakes in the ground was a shock—shock followed by sadness at the loss I knew was coming. With each new foundation, with each new frame wall nailed upright, I could only watch as a little portion of my woods was seized and destroyed.

It was wrong. There were already enough neighbors in the area— we didn't need any more houses pushing into my woods. But there was nothing a ten-year-old kid with a BB gun could do to stop it.

IV.

The days unfold. Their fullness comes upon us, like open sky at dawn. On good days, events land gently. They embed and become one with our landscape, building and nurturing growth. Day by day, the offerings accumulate, layer upon layer. The older become nestled deep within, creating form. The more recent, the most visible, come to rest upon our surface, shaped by that which has come before.

But some days bring hurt. The winds may rise, then tear and break in thunder. Harsh rains can cut, leaving marks. A gulley washes open. More rains send mud and rocks downward, gouging raw a ravine and leaving lowland awash in scattered debris.

Over time, the building up and tearing down scribe us, adorning and carving at our surface.

Third Grade

Mrs. Dunlop was an older teacher. She wasn't mean or nasty or overly strict, but she wasn't as caring as most first and second grade teachers. With third grade came a hint of tougher times that might lie ahead.

Everyone knew that Carl was really smart. School work for him was easy. But the thing that distinguished Carl in my view was not his intelligence, but his drinking skills. I couldn't understand how he could drink so much. After each bathroom break Mrs. Dunlop lined up boys and girls single file at the drinking fountain in the hallway. Everyone took a drink, and then the class returned to the classroom. Most kids drank for about ten seconds--but not Carl. When his turn came Carl would bend over, turn on the drinking fountain and begin sucking in water. And he would keep drinking and drinking. It went on for thirty or forty seconds--sometimes even longer. Carl had been drinking like this since kindergarten.

"How does he do it?" I often wondered. "How does he drink that much all the time?" He wasn't a big kid and he wasn't fat, and so he shouldn't have been able to drink so much more than others. But he did. Adding to the mystery, none of the teachers ever told him to hurry up—it was as if he had a free pass to drink as long as he wanted.

Well, one day it finally hit me. I was standing in line waiting my turn, watching Carl drink, and I realized—"He's not really drinking! He's just holding his lips in the stream of water and not swallowing! He's just pretending." It was a revelation. I had figured him out.

So when my turn came to get a drink, I turned the handle and took my normal drink. And then I stopped swallowing and just held my lips in the flowing water for a few extra seconds, to test my new insight. The technique worked perfectly. Mystery solved.

I never said anything to Carl about his tricky drinking—I knew what was going on, and that was enough for me. I don't know why he did it—maybe it was just a game, or maybe he liked to hold up the line, or maybe he wanted to delay our return to the classroom. With three bathroom breaks a day, over the course of that year Carl probably reduced our classroom time at least a couple hours. For that, maybe I should have thanked him.

Whatever Carl's motives might have been, with that revelation a little something in me woke up. It dawned on me that some people might not play by the normal rules. They had their own way of doing things, and I might have to watch out.

A year or so later Carl took some tests in the principal's office, and the school decided he was so smart that he should skip a grade— Carl found an even better way to reduce his time in class. As for me, I just kept turning on the fountain, drinking what I needed, and letting the next person in line have his turn.

Bobby and I were good friends. He lived in the neighborhood, and we played together all the time—exploring the woods, playing baseball, climbing trees and catching crayfish. Part of being friends meant that every few months we'd have a fight. We'd get into a huff about something, punch each other a few times and go home. After a couple days we'd make up and resume our normal activities.

Mrs. Dunlop didn't understand this. So when she saw Bobby and me fighting on the playground one afternoon, she broke it up, marched us into the classroom and bawled us out. She didn't care who started it or what the fight was about—each of us was at fault. It hadn't been a knock-down, drag-out affair—just some harmless pushing and shoving and broken punches. So our punishment wasn't severe. It was more her promise of what would happen the next time—"If I <u>ever</u> see you fighting again...." We had to stay inside during recess the rest of the week—Bobby seated at a desk on one side of the room and I separated on the other. Within a day or two we were friends again. But I had learned another important lesson. There were ways things worked at home, but a different set of rules could apply at school.

PTA Parents Night came two or three times a year. The first PTA night in the fall was the most important. On that PTA night Carol, Nancy and I had to stay home with a babysitter so Mom and Dad could go to school. Parents Night was their chance to meet your teacher, spend a half hour or so in your classroom, and glimpse your world at school. In the days leading up to PTA night, teachers made you clean out and reorganize your desk and work on special assignments and reports. Some of that work was posted on classroom walls for general viewing, and some was placed on your desktop for parents to look over when they inspected your area.

I thought it was good for parents to see a little of what school was about. And it was probably a good thing for teachers to be reminded that you had parents—reminded that teachers weren't completely in control of your life. But I was a little uncomfortable with PTA night, with parents and teachers talking with each other, comparing notes about me.

I trusted Mom and Dad, but I wondered what they said about me during PTA night. What did they tell the teacher? And what was Mrs. Dunlop telling my parents about me? I wanted to know. I didn't have anything to hide, but whatever they were talking about seemed like my business, too. So when Mom and Dad returned from PTA, I always quizzed them about their conversations at school. They answered my questions, but afterward I was never quite sure I got the whole story.

The best way to deal with girls was to ignore them. Ignoring came naturally. Girls had their own world of dress up and Terri Lee dolls, barrettes and hair brushes, tap dance and ponies—their world held no appeal for boys. So the Kathy's, Beverly's and Barbara's clumped together on the playground, moved in pairs and small groupings on the school bus, and formed their little circles in the cafeteria at lunch time. These were private "Girls Only" clubs--no boys welcome. Signs weren't needed to announce that rule. So we boys separately moved about, our movements tuned to chases and races, bragging about high-flying kites, swapping baseball cards or arguing about the number of Mexicans in Santa Anna's army at the Alamo.

Teachers used these forces to control behavior. "Class, line up boy-girl-boy-girl" was every grade school teacher's command when students left the classroom. The order neutralized her charges, insulating each of us, like rubber around a copper wire.

As long as the groups remained separate, insulated in ignoring mode, an uneasy peace prevailed. But daily activities brushed boys against girls. On the playground the result was group taunting-- "You girls don't even know how many innings there are in a game."

Girls countered taunting with condescension—they had a smooth instinct for it. "Oh, who cares about your silly game? Why don't you boys just get out of here and leave us alone." And they'd raise their noses in haughty disgust as they turned away.

On the school bus, the charges were pressed into close quarters. With no teachers to control the energy, sparks often broke out. Things could flare up quickly.

Paul might start it. "Hey there, Darlene ... I see you got on your ugly green coat again today. You know, you look like a frog in that coat."

Darlene would counter. "Why don't you be quiet." A short pause, then she hit back. "Besides, I wouldn't talk if I was you—with those big ears of yours sticking out—they make you look like a donkey."

"Oh yeah?!" Paul thought for a moment. "Well, at least I don't go around croaking all day—ribbit ribbit ribbit. That's what you sound like—a croaky frog--ribbit ribbit."

"You just better shut up!" Darlene's words were sharp.

"Froggy Legs—that's what we should call you from now on—yeah, that's it … Froggy Legs!" Paul pointed at her knees. "Hey, Tommy, look! Darlene's got skinny little Froggy Legs."

The insults were sincere. They came from within and were meant to hurt.

Eventually the bus would arrive at Paul's stop. He'd give Darlene one last dirty look as he passed forward and then clambered down the steps. The driver closed the door behind Paul, and another daily round of name calling would come to an end.

Heavy churning of the bus motor and the strain of lugging gears now replaced insults, as the school bus began to move and then lumber off down the road. Amid those still on board, in the wake of fresh taunting and insults, the two camps would silently pull back, retreating once again to the uneasy peace of ignoring.

It's surprising what little we remember. All those hours in class, learning the states and the rivers, the capitals and the crops, the lakes and the oceans and the seas…. It all landed somewhere, but eventually the facts fade. So years later the clearest thing that remains is the phrase every third grader memorized to spell the word "geography" correctly: "George Edison's Old Grandmother Rode A Pig Home Yesterday."

Gone Fishing

Sunday school stories at the Methodist Church were the same as the stories at the Presbyterian Church. But the Methodists went on more picnics, pancake breakfasts and cook outs. In Mill Creek Park in Youngstown you could eat Methodist hot dogs with mustard and climb big rocks on the hillside behind the pavilion where everyone gathered. Sometimes the boys and dads would play softball together. At one cook out in Firestone Park in Columbiana, the Methodists had foot races and prizes for kids. For being the fastest boy, I won a brand new, blue fiberglass fishing pole and reel—a big step up over my old bamboo pole back home.

I liked the Methodist moms and dads. Methodist grownups seemed interested in you, even though you were only a kid. Theirs wasn't the same kind of interest as your own Mom or Dad directed at you—Mom and Dad were mostly worried about little things, like if your hair was combed or your shirt was tucked in. Instead, in the hallway at church on Sunday mornings the Manchester's and Neff's, the McKnight's and Wolboldt's talked with you in a way that made you feel welcome and important. So our family joined the Methodists and sometimes attended Sunday services at the tan brick and brown stone church beside the village green.

The summer after third grade, the church presented a thick King James Bible to each kid in my Sunday school class. Inside the front cover they printed your full name and the date in fancy ink lettering. I brought the Bible home and placed it on a shelf in my room. I didn't read it very much—the blue fishing pole got a lot more use. But it seemed important to keep the weighty book in your possession. It wasn't the sort of thing you could just forget about.

Cub Scouts

Grownups sold Cub Scouts as a club for boys--the allure of fun times with friends, the promise of interesting meetings, serious oaths, uniforms and badges, Indian lore, solemn pledges and patriotic scouting activities. But it wasn't boys—it was moms who actually ran things.

The den was the basic unit of Cub Scouts. Each den was led by a Den Mother—a well-meaning, neighborhood mom who volunteered to run the program for her son's friends. Her instincts guided Cub Scouting.

Scouting began about third grade. Once a week after returning home from school, a half dozen Cub Scouts from the neighborhood pedaled to Mellinger Road for our den meeting. We met at a home near the edge of the woods that contained the hollow tree with steps nailed up the inside. You might expect a tree of that significance to figure into Cub Scout meeting activities from time to time. But it never did. Instead, our meetings were usually filled with arts and crafts projects—cobbling together attic relics for the future.

39

One of those projects was a Cub Scout ashtray, a gift each Scout would present to his Mom on Mother's Day. The main part of the ashtray was a plaster cast of a Cub Scout, about three inches tall. The cast of the scout was just from the stomach up—like a bust of a famous general or president you might see in a museum. I carefully painted my scout's blue and yellow neckerchief, his glossy blue uniform with red, yellow and white patches and badges, decorative yellow lines on his cap, his brown hair and all his facial features. The next week, when the paint was dry, we glued the bust to a small, curved ¾ inch plywood base. Beside the bust was a circular hole in the base that held a small glass ashtray. A couple weeks later, after all the coats of varnish on the plywood dried, I took the finished piece home and gave it to Mom.

Mom and Dad didn't smoke, but we had a couple ashtrays around the house for occasional guests. Mom displayed my ashtray on an end table in the living room. In the bright light under the lamp, the Cub Scout ashtray gleamed fresh and official.

The thought that smoking killed people never crossed our minds.

One fall meeting our Den Mother proposed a good project--paper mache masks for Halloween. A trick-or-treating project—now that was more like it!

First I had to decide on a Halloween costume. I liked my bum outfit from last year—one of Dad's beat up jackets and baggy work pants and a beard smudged across my face with blackened cork. But you couldn't wear the same outfit as last year—I needed something different. Whatever outfit I chose had to look real—people had to know what I was. I decided to be Donald Duck.

Week by week my Donald Duck creation took shape at Cub Scouts. To start, I blew up a big balloon until it was about a foot and a half tall—the shape of a head. Then I covered the balloon with a thick coat of paper mache—strips of newspaper soaked in a gooey flour paste. To the head shape, I added more newspaper strips to form Donald's beak and on top, his round sailor's hat. It took a lot of paper mache to do that—the mask weighed seven or eight pounds. By the next den meeting, the balloon head had dried

40

and hardened. So I popped and removed the balloon and carved a hole in the base so I could stick my head inside. Next I cut two little round eye holes in the front of the mask over the beak. I painted the head white for feathers, the beak orange and the hat blue, and drew big duck eyes around the peep holes. By the following week the paint had dried, so I took the mask home. There I added a black ribbon around the base of the hat—a finishing touch to make Donald really true-to-life. There was no mistaking that it was Donald Duck.

I was pleased with my duck head. But in the days leading up to Halloween, I became concerned that a part of my costume hadn't received enough attention. Once I placed Donald overtop my head, there was way too much room inside. The base of the head rested on my shoulders, but there was nothing to hold the head upright— it was unstable. Sometimes the mask would tilt forward, banging me in the back of the head, and then flop backwards, pushing up against my nose. I should have figured out a way to keep it in place. But I thought, "It's not too bad. I'll just hold the mask a little if I need to. It'll be OK."

When I ran out of the house Halloween evening to join Bobby and Richy trick-or-treating, I had barely left the yard before the problem really hit. Every time I took a step Donald's head flopped around— jouncing me inside when it moved and making it hard to see out through the eye holes. When the head wasn't banging around, the weight of the beak tilted it forward, aiming my view down to a little area two feet in front of me. I had been standing still when I tested my mask before Halloween—keeping it upright then was just a nuisance. But trying to run with it on was a serious problem.

Trick-or-treating lasted only a couple hours—just so much time to cover all the ground. To hit the houses on Meadowview, Pleasant Valley and Mellinger would require a lot of running. And even at a fast pace, we might not have time to reach the scattered houses up on Raccoon we also had targeted, since they gave good treats. Halloween was all about candy—the four inch Tootsie Rolls, packs of Necco Wafers, handfuls of Atomic Fireballs and small cartons of M&M's. Big five cent candy bars were best—on a good night you might get thirty or forty Hershey bars, Snickers, Three Musketeers, Nestle bars and Mounds. Halloween was all about coming home at the end of the evening and spreading that candy across the kitchen table, tallying up your loot. Any limitation on running could seriously reduce my candy haul.

But now the race was on, and there was no stopping it. The bands of ghosts and goblins, witches and princesses had begun their wandering. The ringing of doorbells and buzzers was prompting porch lights to flick on and front doors to swing open. Calls of "Trick-or-Treat" were rising from the twilight, like the fading chirping of fall crickets. No more time for costume work—Trick-or-Treating had begun.

So I did the only thing possible—I tried to keep up as best I could. With one hand I held Donald and the other I clutched the candy bag, my narrow vision bouncing around like a bumpy movie camera. I followed Richy and the pack from door to door. When I ran, my duck head jostled and bounced from side to side, and the edges of the heavy mask hurt my shoulders. When I stopped to stand at an open door to collect candy, I needed both hands to hold my candy bag open, and so my mask tilted one way or the other. If it tilted down, I saw only the shoes of the person giving treats. If it went up, I could only see the top of the door frame. As the evening darkened, it was harder to see where I was going, to avoid bushes, ditches and mailboxes at the end of driveways. I ran holding Donald's big head upright with both hands, one on each side to steady it, with my candy bag banging against my chest. Donald was a major headache.

I kept up, but at a price. By the end of the night, when the neighbors up on Raccoon opened their front doors to our tired announcements of "Trick-or-Treat," on their doorstep stood a wobbly Donald Duck holding his head. No one offered aspirin instead of chocolate.

In the days after Halloween, Donald stayed in my room—on the floor against the wall near my bed. But he took up a lot of space, began getting in the way and just collected dust. Eventually I carted Donald upstairs and placed him at rest on some boxes in the corner of the attic—one of those important, useless things you don't quite know what to do with anymore. A few years later, my ashtray would follow Donald into the attic.

Baseball

Isolated on Palmyra Road, with no boys nearby, baseball games weren't possible. But with our move to Pleasant Valley, there were now friends within bicycle distance. And up on the corner of Meadowview Drive and Raccoon Road was a baseball field.

A beat up backstop stood behind home plate. The rusty chain link fence was about eight feet long and six feet tall, with a couple holes where the metal squares had been broken and bent apart. On one end along the ground the chain link was curled up, opening a gap where the ball sometimes knocked through. But the backstop worked to catch most pitches. Our diamond wasn't much--home plate, the bases and the pitcher's mound were lop-sided dirt clearings where the infield grass and weeds had been stomped down. We used a big stone or spare ball glove to better mark first. The outfield sloped away toward left and center, but not enough of a tilt to be a problem. Assorted grasses, patches of dandelions and broadleaf weeds covered the field—I think it was a hayfield in earlier years. But it was a big, open lot, with no houses nearby or trees to get in the way. Mr. Kaufel, who owned the field, must have had a soft spot for neighborhood kids, for he had his son in high school mow back the weeds every couple of weeks to keep the field playable.

I played baseball because I liked it.

On summer days, I'd put on my jeans, T-shirt, tennis shoes and ball cap, get my Warren Spahn glove, ball and favorite bat, and pedal up Meadowview to the field. Usually there were just three of us—Richy, Bobby and I. But that was enough to play a game of baseball. We'd pick a permanent pitcher (say, Richy), one team (say, me) would take the outfield, and the other team (Bobby) would be up to bat. The batter could fly out to the pitcher or fielder, and that would be an out. If the batter hit a grounder to me, I'd throw it to Richy, and he'd cover the bases and the plate. If the batter was safe, we'd put an imaginary runner on that base, and Bobby would return to the batter's box for the next at bat. There was no stealing, and you could force out imaginary runners. With only two guys in the field, sometimes it took a while to get three outs, but we always did.

Playing baseball on Meadowview was about playing. It was about fun, the feel of a hard swing of the bat, throwing and catching a scuffed up ball, sprinting to first on the crack of the bat. It was about the feeling of confidence when an easy fly ball came my direction, knowing that I could get under it and snag it right in that center, worn spot in my glove.

And so summer days would pass, as we played out the innings, pitching and hitting, chasing imaginary runners, wearing out baseballs and arguing safe or out. Looking back, it's clear we were all safe. I'd like to imagine that somehow the three of us could have gone on forever playing our simple game in that field. But we couldn't. Come next spring, Little League would arrive and change the game of baseball.

Graduating to Little League was a big step. Canfield had half a dozen teams, each with a coach, a roster of more than enough players for each position, and a weekly practice and game schedule. The ball field was in town off Lisbon Street, angled between tall woods along the left field line and about two hundred yards from the Erie Railroad station out toward right. The field had everything—a couple sets of bleachers for fans behind home plate, tall wire netting to protect spectators, dugouts, a level dirt infield that we would smooth before games, pitcher's mound, real bases to strap down at first, second and third, a chest high wooden home run fence, scoreboard out beyond left field, chalk to mark the foul lines and batter's box, and a little shanty behind the bleachers where they sold bottles of pop, snacks and candy bars during games. And there were official uniforms, white with colored letters across your chest advertising the team sponsor (I was on McCabe Drug) with matching hat and socks. And real black leather baseball shoes, with steel cleats to dig into the dirt.

The league was run by dads, but it was for kids. Come April, every day at school Little League players talked about the next practice, the results of the big games at the field the night before, who struck out or got a double, and how your team was always going to beat your friend's team in the next game.

I came to learn the coaches followed an unspoken hierarchy in assigning players to positions—the best players were usually the pitcher and the catcher (since they had to handle the ball the most), followed by the infielders. After that, coaches put the best outfielder in left (because most kids batted right and solid hits went left), followed by center field. Finally the weakest player would be put in right field, where he could do the least amount of damage. I played right field.

It didn't bother me that I played there. I wasn't a bad player, but I was scrawny and probably didn't inspire much confidence with the coach. OK, so maybe I didn't see a lot line drives and fly balls coming my way. But I could back up throws to first and come in on soft grounders that dribbled through the infield. And I could add my voice to the mandatory "Hey batter batter batter batter SWING batter!" chant which filled the field every pitch. I was fine with that.

One evening after dinner Dad encouraged me to practice pitching a little. He seemed to think that I might be good at it. I wasn't so sure, but Dad got out his J.C. Higgins Nellie Fox flat ball glove, and for a few weeks in the evenings we'd go out into the yard. He'd catch while I practiced my windup and delivery. In Little League, pitching wasn't much about curveballs and sliders, knuckle balls and changeups. Instead it was mostly about trying to get the ball somewhere close to the plate without hitting the batter. And Dad was right--I wasn't too bad at that. But I didn't feel like a pitcher, and so I didn't mention to the coach that Dad and I had been working at it. I figured that someday, if I got good enough, I'd say something to the coach, and maybe he would let me throw a few during batting practice. We would see how it went. I was in no hurry. There was plenty of time for me to become a great pitcher.

At a game some weeks later, McCabe Drug was getting clobbered. From my vantage point out in right, I had watched as the other team knocked two of our pitchers out of the game, built up an impossible lead, and now our third pitcher was struggling to get one more out to end the inning and keep the infield full of runners from crossing home. As I looked to the infield, waiting for the next batter to come to the plate, I noticed Dad standing beside the end of our dugout talking with the coach. I thought about it for a second and had an uneasy feeling. Then another pitch, the batter swung, and when the dust settled yet another run had scored and the bases were still loaded. The coach left the dugout, signaled time out to the umpire, and instead of walking to the pitcher's mound he turned and came jogging out to right field, straight at me. "Uh oh," I thought.

"Your Dad says you've been practicing some pitching," the coach said. I told him we had. "Do you want to give it a try?" and he motioned toward the pitcher's mound.

As I think back about that conversation, I guess I was given a choice. But with the coach standing there in the middle of right field and Dad watching from near the dugout, I felt like there was only one answer to the question. "OK," I said.

As I left the outfield and stepped onto the infield, I felt I was wandering into a foreign territory, someplace I shouldn't be entering and didn't belong. Fans in the stands and the rest of my team on the field were watching, wondering—"What's Gentzel doing there? He's not a pitcher?! What's going on?" But I trod over to the mound, picked up the ball, stepped on the rubber, and got ready to take a few warm ups.

A lot of the fun of Little League was the customs governing intimidation of opposing players. These traditions were developed over decades, passed on from year to year, and honed to perfection by Little Leaguers each season. Second only to the mandatory chatter rule was the rule governing behavior of players in the dugout watching an opposing pitcher warm up. The rule required players to observe a moment of silence with the first warm up pitch, and then erupt into howls of glee and derisive laughter about how they're gonna kill him when they get up to bat. So I went through my windup and threw that first warm up pitch, sparking joyous whoops from the opposing dugout. It wasn't a bad pitch—it might even have been a strike. And their laughter bothered me some. But it bothered me more that Donny, our catcher, then fired the ball back to me faster than my pitch had come at him, as if to say "Come on, THROW the darn thing!" So I reared back and threw a few more at him, each time to the laughter and cat calls of the other dugout. Then the umpire shouted "Play ball!"

There were two outs, the bases were loaded, and all eyes were on me. As I stood center stage with the ball, I watched the batter settle into his stance, my heart was pounding, and I sure missed right field. But there was no turning back. So I eyed down the batter, began my windup, drew back hard, and let it fly. The ball headed for the plate, high and inside. The batter swung and popped it up. Seconds later our third baseman caught it, and the next moment I was running with the rest of the team back to our dugout amid shouts of "Way to go, Gentzel!" I remember thinking, "Gee, only one pitch. That wasn't hard."

McCabe Drug may have scored a run during our at bats that inning, though it didn't really matter--the score was hopeless. But the game wasn't over--there was another inning to play. I soon realized I was going to have to leave the safety of the dugout and go back out there. And this time I wasn't going to get away with just one pitch.

With our third out, the coach told us to take the field again. I faced up to what I had to do, marched out to the pitcher's mound and threw a few more warm ups. I was a long way from feeling confident, but somewhere inside there was a flicker of hope that maybe, just maybe, I could get through this.

From that point forward, my memory of the contest is muddled. Whatever the game had been up to then, it abruptly turned into a sort of out-of-body experience, the kind of feeling you have when hurled into a life-threatening catastrophe or collision where you feel yourself separated from your body, watching it career uncontrollably toward certain doom. They clobbered me. They pummeled out a barrage of hits and walks, on and on, running endlessly around the bases, and with each crack of the bat I had to fight harder and harder to hold back the tears. Finally I couldn't stop them. I threw the ball then wiped my eyes between pitches, then threw and wiped again. When the coach finally realized his pitcher was crying, he walked out to me and mercifully ended it.

After that, Dad and I didn't practice pitching any more. Next game I was back in right field.

I stuck with Little League. It was July, a couple years later and baseball season was nearing an end. Through spring and early summer, my game was improving—especially my hitting. I was getting respectable in swinging to meet the ball, driving it far enough over the infielders, and sprinting to first for a single. Oh, I might dream about hitting a home run. But as small as I was, I couldn't hit for power. Some guys, like my friend Bobby from Pleasant Valley, were just bigger and could hit the ball over the fence. I knew I wasn't one of them and had come to accept that.

My longest hits in Little League were long foul balls, way outside the left field line. Actually, it was way outside the left field, period. I liked pitches inside, and sometimes I would swing far too early, sending the ball sailing over the third base dugout, beyond the edge of the ball field into the nearby trees. It was hard for me to hold back on my swing.

That July evening when I came up to bat, the game wasn't on the line. I think we were comfortably ahead, had a man on second, and there was only one out. I was hoping to advance him with a hit into the outfield. I walked to the batter's box, and set up beside the plate. The umpire, dressed in black and hidden away behind his mask, had just finished sweeping dust from the plate. He stuffed the little brush into his back pocket as he turned and stepped back into position behind the catcher. "Play ball!"

Early in the count, the second or third pitch, the ball came fast, waist high over the inside corner, and I swung. Bat met ball and I took off, watching the line drive head out the left field line—it was a solid shot, heading straight down the line. And it carried and carried, aiming right for the foul pole that rose above the home run fence. As I neared first and turned to watch the flight of the ball, I was amazed to see the ball clear the fence by a few inches, just inside the foul pole. I hit a home run! I tagged first and looked again to the outfield to be sure. The left fielder was standing out by the foul pole, looking beyond the fence, and the ball was nowhere to be seen. I had really hit a home run! The guys in the dugout let out a cheer. So I slowed down to a jog and rounded second. An honest-to-goodness home run! I was approaching third when I realized something was wrong.

The home plate umpire had walked out toward third and was motioning to me to go back. I slowed and stopped. I was confused. The coach came out of the dugout and walked to the umpire. They talked for a little bit and then the coach turned from the umpire toward me and told me to go back to second. The umpire had called it a ground rule double, not a home run. He said that the ball went THROUGH the fence, not over it?! The fence was made of vertical, wooden slats about four feet tall, with a narrow space between each slat. The ump must have thought the ball smashed through one of those spaces. He was wrong—I saw the ball had clearly gone over the fence. I was robbed! But in those days you didn't argue, and so I turned around and went silently back to second.

Afterward everybody said it was a home run—my team, guys on the other team, parents in the bleachers—everybody. I was over by the snack shed after the game, and one of the older players, Tim, was there drinking a bottle of pop. Tim played catcher on one of the other teams and was really good. He could hit home runs. Since he was a grade ahead of me at school and above me in the pecking order, normally I wouldn't talk to him. But he was talking to another kid about my hit. I awkwardly joined in, telling them what I saw, and how it was definitely a homer. We spoke for a few minutes, and Tim finally looked at me and concluded, "Well, that was a home run in my book." I didn't need to hear anything else. Forget what the darn umpire said—Tim's judgment was good enough for me.

Dos and Don'ts

There were a lot of layers to sort through in dealing with girls. There was the ignoring layer, where you just minded your own business and left them alone. Beneath that layer was the uneasy peace, the tension that could break through into insults. To protect yourself, you had to know how to manage those layers. Then somewhere along the way, another layer began to emerge. At first you had no idea something was happening. But over time it grew and asserted itself. It was the girlfriend layer, and along with it came a whole new set of complications.

There was no rhyme or reason to it. The dislike boys felt toward snooty girls in their Girls Only club was real. But little by little, from somewhere among the crowds in school, a special girl emerged, and she seemed different. It didn't matter that her interests were at

49

odds with yours, or that she ignored you, or that she could be snooty with the best of them. What came to matter was that you were interested in her. And it was impossible to ignore her because you liked her.

The most important thing about having a girlfriend was that you had to keep it a secret. Anyone branded as a boyfriend or girlfriend instantly became an object of ridicule. The teasers would come circling in from everywhere--even your friends would join in. And unlike the insults on the bus, this teasing didn't end when the bus stopped at your home. It would start again the next morning when the bus picked you up, and it could go on for days--until both guilty parties had been completely humiliated and all the glee of the teasers was spent. Self-defense required that you pretend to ignore the one girl you couldn't. The deception hardened you.

We all knew not to lie. But if someone caught on to your secret and accused you of having a girlfriend, you'd deny it. If the accusations kept coming, you'd lie again and again--as long as it took and with as much conviction as the situation required. And not once did those lies prompt the slightest twinge of remorse.

"You NEVER hit a girl! Do you understand me!?" Mom was staring at me. Her pointed finger aimed right between my eyes. "Never EVER hit a girl!" She meant business. "Now, you go apologize to your sister."

I knew the rule—I had heard it many times before from Mom, and I almost always followed it. But summer vacation was dragging on, my sisters and I had been spending too much time together, and we were getting on each other's nerves. That morning Nancy was picking at me and teasing about something—and she just wouldn't stop. I warned her, but she was in one of those moods. She didn't pay any attention to my warnings, and just kept it up. Finally I lost my temper and hauled off and slugged her good on the shoulder, and she went crying to Mom.

So Mom bawled me out and I apologized to Nancy. Afterwards, even though Nancy deserved it, I was sorry I hit her.

One hot day later that summer, Mom gave Nancy and me a few dollars for admission to Sunnybrook, the local swimming pool. The pool was off Raccoon Road, about a ten minute walk from home. It was sheltered behind a grouping of shade trees, at the end of a wooded lane through a field. Nancy and I rolled our swimsuits into a couple of big bath towels and headed off toward the pool.

Sunnybrook wasn't a typical rectangular pool, the kind with a shallow end and a diving board at the deep end. Instead it was a big oval, with gently sloping sides all around—no drop offs. The sides and bottom were covered with concrete painted sky blue. The pool was for younger kids—the water was only about four feet at the deepest. But the water was cool, with plenty of room to splash and swim.

The pool was crowded that day, filled with dozens of noisy kids, inflatable life rafts, rubber nose plugs, leaky snorkeling masks and droopy, dripping swimsuits. A lady lifeguard watched over swimmers from a grassy area above the sloping sides. The constant splashing and thrashing in the pool against the bright glare of sun on the water made hers a difficult watch.

Nancy and I didn't swim together—we were too old for that. We went our separate ways in the pool. But Mom's instruction over the years to "Be careful" had sunk in, and so from time to time we looked around the water to check up on each other. I was over by the side of the pool and Nancy was off toward the middle when I noticed some kid come up to her. I didn't know him. He stopped, stood in front of her and said something. Nancy said something back. I couldn't hear them--the din of the pool drowned out their words. Then for some reason he splashed Nancy a couple times and pushed her. Nancy righted herself, and she splashed right back. Then he grabbed her and pushed again. I didn't know what they were scuffling about, but he was bigger and she was in trouble.

I started her way. Then the kid grabbed her again and tried to force her down in the water, and she struggled against him. I took off through the crowded pool toward the commotion, running and splashing my way at the kid. I was on him before he saw me coming, and when I met him I punched and yanked at him. He backed off Nancy and she got loose and moved away. Then I punched some more.

51

We were shoving and pushing at each other when I heard the lifeguard yelling. "Stop that fighting! You! Get out of the pool!" The lady lifeguard was standing by the edge, pointing at me and the kid, "Out of the pool!" she directed. I stopped struggling and so did the kid. Nearby swimmers quieted and stepped back. I paused a few seconds to catch my breath, and then began pushing through the water toward the lady. The fight was over.

The kid and I stood poolside before the lifeguard and received our scolding. She pointed toward the big sign on the bath house with all the pool rules—No Fighting. She gave us a good lecture and then told the kid and me to stay out of the water—my swim was over. Not long after that Nancy and I rolled up our towels and walked home.

Mom had never told me it was OK to hit boys—she always discouraged my getting into fights with anyone. Nor was I told I was expected to come to the aid of my sisters if they were in trouble—we never had that conversation, either. Of course I knew you weren't supposed to fight at the pool—I knew the rules. But when I saw Nancy being pushed around, I didn't think about anybody's rules or expectations—none of that entered my mind. I just went after that kid, and I was glad I did.

Some rules don't need posting poolside—they just happen.

Fourth Grade

The lists posted outside the office told me I was assigned to Mrs. Carlemagno's class. Mike, Jimmy, Jackie, Larry, Jane Ann and a number of other familiar kids were also assigned to her class. But Mrs. Carlemagno was new to Canfield—none of us had any idea what she was like. Our fourth grade classroom was also a departure from what we knew. We left the 1920's section of the school building and moved into the newest section, the two-story tan brick addition on the opposite side of the bus circle.

Carol, Nancy and I were out early to the bus stop that first day of school. With Bobby from down the street and a couple other neighborhood kids, we waited for Bus 9 to come down Meadowview, load up at our corner, turn left on Pleasant Valley and continue on its route. The ride to school, with all the stops, would be about twenty-five minutes. We waited, all of us a little uneasy with first day jitters.

Number 9 was reliable; throughout third grade it had always arrived within a five-minute window. But that morning the window came and went, and no Bus Number 9. We figured things were probably off a bit with some expected confusion on the first day. It would be by soon. So we waited some more. Five minutes stretched to ten minutes, then to fifteen. Mom had been checking on us from the front door, and when twenty minutes came and went, that was long enough. We packed up into the car, and Mom drove us to school.

When we pulled up to school, all was quiet out front—the buses had come and gone, and kids were inside. We got out of the car, and Mom drove away. We walked to the office and told one of the office ladies our story--the driver probably made a wrong turn somewhere on his route. Since we had a good excuse for being late, the woman told us to go to our respective classes and just tell the teachers what happened.

Mrs. Carlemagno was in front, talking to the class when I walked in. She was young, slender, with dark hair clipped short in a no nonsense style. I walked up to her, interrupting her talk. I explained how my bus hadn't come, and she asked my name. Then she motioned to my empty desk and told me to go sit down. She resumed her talk as I went to my desk, sat, tilted open my desktop and placed fresh papers, notebooks and pencils inside.

The class was filling out some first day forms with names and addresses and phone numbers. All of my #2 pencils were brand new and hadn't been sharpened yet. So I grabbed a couple pencils, walked to the pencil sharpener on the side wall, and began sharpening so I could work on the forms.

"Did I tell you that you could use the pencil sharpener?" The voice was forceful. I stopped and looked up. Mrs. Carlemagno was staring at me from across the room.

"Uh, no," I answered. You didn't have to ask to sharpen your pencil in third grade.

"If you want to leave your seat, you ask me. Do you understand?" Her words were clipped, like her hair.

I nodded and said yes.

"Finish sharpening your pencil and sit down," she instructed me. I completed my sharpening and returned to my desk.

It was not a good beginning.

At school, your desk was your home. It was where you belonged, a safe place, like home base during hide-and-seek. Beneath the big formica tilt top was the steel cavity where you kept books and workbooks, papers and pencils and pens, notebooks and crayons and rulers. Your desk required some housekeeping, or else it would fill up with old assignments, worn out pencils, and papers you should have taken home. The desktop and storage cavity were connected to the seat and base by a heavy steel support that angled down next to your right knee. The chair section was made of contoured wood, and the seat was hard but fairly comfortable. It was big enough for sliding a little from side to side, or slouching down and stretching your legs forward to keep from getting too stiff in one position.

Teachers never arranged desks in rows across the room, with students sitting beside each other, elbow-to-elbow. Instead, to reduce interaction among kids, the desks were always arranged in parallel columns, from the front of the room to the back, with an aisle separating each column. As a result, over the course of the school year you became very familiar with the habits of the person seated directly in front of you.

Lemoine sat in front of me. We generally ignored each other, but I got along with her OK enough, even though she was a girl. She was a good student—interested, bright and attentive. But she did have one bad habit. She wore loafers, and often during the day she would rub one foot against the other and slip off her shoes. I guess she was just fidgeting or giving her feet a rest. She'd leave the loafers off for a while--maybe slide them around a little under her desk or under her seat--before finally slipping them back on. This playing with her shoes didn't affect Lemoine's concentration on lessons—she maybe wasn't even aware what her feet were doing.

But I was paying attention. By looking downward over the front edge of my desk and underneath Lemoine's, I could usually see her feet. Normally I was a little curious as to where her shoes were. One afternoon as Mrs. Carlemagno led the class in a history lesson, I saw that Lemoine had both shoes off. Unlike most days where her open shoes rested under her desk, this day one of her shoes had gotten pushed backward, far under her seat, toward me. A little something in me perked up, and I thought, "I wonder if I can slide forward and reach that shoe with my foot." I surveyed the landscape. The teacher was busy conducting her lesson, asking questions of Jane Ann seated near the front of the classroom. All clear. So I slowly slid forward on my seat, slouched down and extended my leg toward the shoe. I reached it. And after one or two tries I succeeded in getting control of the shoe and slowly pulled it back toward me, away from Lemoine's feet. When I had the lone shoe back under my desk, I sat back up straight. No one saw what I had done. I felt pretty clever. I was looking forward to Lemoine's discovering that her shoe was gone, to her realizing she had a problem and then searching around trying to figure out where her shoe went.

Nothing happened for a few minutes--Lemoine didn't poke around for her shoe. So I decided to let Mike in on it. Mike sat across the aisle to my left, the side away from the teacher. So I glanced over at him to get his attention, lowered my left hand below the edge of my desk, and pointed down at the shoe. After several points Mike caught on, saw the shoe, and a big smile came over his face.

Now, Mike was a good friend, and he could keep a secret. But Mike liked to laugh—he liked to laugh a whole lot. And as Mike looked at my stolen shoe and imagined Lemoine's predicament, he started to giggle. At first it was just a little giggle, and he suppressed it. But the giggle started to grow, it became more noticeable, and it began bursting through his smile. Then his head and shoulders started shaking. "OK, come on, quiet down, Mike," I thought. But he couldn't control himself. And the giggle got louder, and Mike's head and shoulders shook more with muffled laughter. I gave him another pained look, urging him to stop, but there was nothing I could do—there was no stopping him now. My little joke was spinning out of control! Mike fought to keep it inside, but all that bottled up laughter shook him hard.

"Mike, would you mind telling the class what's so funny?" Mrs. Carlemagno saw something was going on and interrupted the lesson. Unlike Mike, she was not in a humorous mood. Normally her attention would bring an immediate stop to any laughter, but Mike was too far gone.

He laughed again and then blurted out, "Bobby has Lemoine's shoe!" And he giggled some more. I groaned, wanting to slouch down again and disappear under my desk.

Mike and I got our due for teasing Lemoine and interrupting class. Mrs. Carlemagno knew it wasn't Lemoine's fault—she was the victim, so she wasn't punished. But I did feel a little bad for Lemoine, since her wandering loafer habits were exposed to the world by my wrongdoing. After that, Lemoine did a better job of keeping her shoes on.

Fourth grade curriculum included multiplication table memorization. We started with the easiest--one times one is one, one times two is two, and so on. After we learned our "one times" we turned to "two times"—two times one is two, two times two is four.... From there we progressed to "three times" then over a period of weeks worked our way up to "eight times" and "nine times." With each new series, we also reviewed previous series.

The class performed daily multiplication drills together. Instead of using simple flash cards, Mrs. Carlemagno had devised a clever way of leading our drills. She took a big piece of light blue poster board, about two feet by three feet, and secured it to the front wall near her desk. She wrote down all the digits on the poster board, from 0 to 9, in a big circle. Zero was at the top, and the rest of the numbers, from 1 through 9, were written around the circle like the face of a clock. In the center of the circle she taped a small metal hook where she could hang a "times" cards--one of ten cards, each with a single number on it, from 0 to 9. Each "times" card had a little hole punched at the top so it could be placed on the hook.

To practice our drills, Mrs. Carlemagno would take a "times" card and hang it on the hook—say she picked the number 5. That meant we'd be practicing our "five times." Then she stood beside the poster board and, with a long, wooden stick, pointed at one of the numbers in the circle. If she pointed at 7, that meant 5 times 7, and the class would call out the answer "35." If she pointed at 4, that meant 5 times 4, and we would call out "20." If she wanted to practice "eight times," she'd remove the 5 card from the hook and replace it with 8, and off we'd go with our "eight times" drill.

I applied myself to learning multiplication tables. Most of them weren't too hard. The zero's and the one's and the two's were simple. Ever since I learned to add, I liked the numbers 3 and 5, and so the "three times" and "five times" weren't bad, either. But the six's, seven's and eight's could be confusing. I had to think a little about those.

One day we were seated in class practicing multiplication drills. Mrs. Carlemagno was up front with her pointer, standing next to the blue poster board. She was pointing, the class was calling out the answers, and I was having trouble. Over the last week it was becoming clear to me that I was not keeping up with the rest of the class. When she pointed, I would start to think, but before I could figure out the answer, my thinking was interrupted by the class calling out the response. It was too much noise, and I was always about a half second slower than everyone else. With each day, this was becoming more of a problem.

But that day, in the middle of the drill, an idea occurred to me. Maybe if I put my hands over my ears to keep the noise out, my thinking wouldn't be interrupted, I could concentrate better and I could answer faster. "Why, sure," I thought. "That's a good idea." Discretely, I leaned forward, placed my elbows on the desktop and cradled my head between my hands. Then I plugged up my ears with the ends of my middle fingers and watched Mrs. Carlemagno. We were doing "seven times," and she pointed to the number 8. I thought for a second and called out "56." Then she pointed to 5, I thought for a second and called out "35." I was answering faster--it seemed to be working. Mrs. Carlemagno pointed at more numbers, and with all the noise blocked from my head I sang out the answers. I sensed that my answers were now coming at the same time as the rest of the class. "Good," I thought. "That's all I need—just some quiet so I can think." My plan was working, and I was keeping pace.

Mrs. Carlemagno paused several seconds and said something. But I couldn't hear her. Instead I was intent on watching her get ready to point to another number, so I could respond. She then turned toward the poster board and pointed to the number 6. I thought, "7 times 6 is 42," and I sang out "42!"

The answer had barely left my lips when everyone in class abruptly turned and stared at me. Lemoine, Jane Ann, Jack and the kids in front twisted around to look, the kids beside me all drew back—their faces surprised--and Mrs. Carlemagno lowered her pointer and her eyes fixed on me. What did I do? My hands dropped from my head.

In that same instant I realized what happened. Sometimes Mrs. Carlemagno called on just one person to answer alone, to test his skill—usually someone having trouble. In her pause, she must have called on someone, and I hadn't heard her. So I had just disobeyed her, yelled out the answer overtop some poor kid, and everyone probably thought I was being a big smarty-pants show off. Mike forced a whisper at me from across the aisle, "What are you doing?!" I cringed and shrugged, speechless. I had not foreseen my plan's fatal flaw.

The next move was Mrs. Carlemagno's. The room was silent, and she looked at me for a long while ... the calm before the storm. I expected the worst. Maybe I'd get sent home or sent to the principal's office, or maybe even get paddled. Something terrible was coming for sure. But after a long stare, she simply turned away, quietly raised her pointer to the poster board and said, "All right, class, let's continue." The class turned around and faced the front of the room. "Huh?" I thought. "She didn't say anything?!" Then Mrs. Carlemagno pointed to another number, and the class proceeded with our "seven times" drill. I was shocked! She didn't say a thing…. I couldn't believe it.

I don't know why Mrs. Carlemagno decided to ignore my outburst. Maybe somehow she understood what happened, why I shouted out the answer. Or maybe by then she knew me well enough and just expected me to do stupid things. I don't know. After that, she never said a word to me about it, and I sure as heck didn't bring it up with her, either.

Arithmetic has lots of rules—like how to borrow from columns on the left when you subtract, the rule about carrying from the ones to the tens when you add and how to bring down figures from the dividend in long division. That day I learned a new one--keep your fingers out of your ears when multiplying.

Once past those early trials with Mrs. Carlemagno, fourth grade improved. In time she and I grew to accept one another. I tried to do the right thing most of the time, and I think she came to see that. She was a good teacher. I was reminded of it every time I heard the kids next door in Mrs. Sturmire's fourth grade class getting screamed at. Her yelling would come shaking through the walls and echoing in through the hallway door. In those shouts, you knew some poor kid next door was getting it, and everyone—even Mrs. Carlemagno--held their breath until the storm in the next room died down. Mrs. Carlemagno didn't scream.

Jack and I became good friends. We began collecting Lincoln head pennies, so each day we compared dates and mint marks discovered in our Dads' change the previous evening. The 1909-S VDB became the holy grail of coin collecting that year. Our quest went unfulfilled, but the search was exciting. Comic books were preferred literature, and the mailman's delivery of the latest Walt Disney's Comics and Stories triggered monthly reviews with Jack of Mickey and Goofy's newest adventure.

I couldn't be angry with Mike about Lemoine's shoe—Mike was just being Mike. When he wasn't laughing, Mike lived on a strict diet of baseball. By fourth grade many of us were becoming too sophisticated to wear our Little League baseball caps to school. But not Mike—he wore his proudly all year. The World Series in the fall and the arrival of Little League in spring were cornerstone events of the year. If it hadn't been for my fabled head bonk episode that spring, the rest of fourth grade would have been pretty good.

It began innocently enough one lunch time. Each lunch period the fourth grade classrooms merged and kids with lunches from home gathered in a single classroom to eat under the supervision of one of the fourth grade teachers. The other teacher on lunch duty led a long parade of fourth grade cafeteria kids through the junior high and senior high halls the length of the school to the cafeteria. They ate there; then the parade returned to the classrooms when lunch was through.

My friends and I were part of the lunch box group that remained in the classroom. Each room had an army green steel trash can, about two feet tall, where you threw away your wax paper, orange peels and cellophane when you were done. To eliminate foul smells of pickle juice and leftover peanut butter in the room that afternoon, a janitor always came by near the end of lunch period to carry off the trash can to the cafeteria for disposal. That day several of us were slower than usual eating, and when we walked over to the trash can, it was gone--the janitor had already been by. So we told Mrs. Carlemagno our problem, and she OK'd four of us to walk over to the cafeteria and throw our trash away, all by ourselves. That sounded like fun.

It was a pleasant spring day, so we exited the building and ran across the bus circle toward the side door of the cafeteria. Inside we found a big trash can and tossed in our leftovers. Mission accomplished. Lunch was winding down, and inside the cafeteria Mrs. Sturmire was assembling the fourth grade lunch parade for the walk back to class. We could have joined the group, but she didn't notice us. Plus, we were feeling a little special and wanted to continue by ourselves. Rather than going back the way we came, we decided to return via the inside halls. So we left the cafeteria, walked across the underpass, and entered the high school section of the building.

From that point, there were two ways back to fourth grade—via the first floor or via the second. From the very first day of fourth grade the rule was "Never Use the Second Floor." The second floor was for upperclassmen, it was off limits, we weren't allowed there. The fourth grade cafeteria parade always traveled the first floor. So of course when the four of us came to the foot of the steps, Mike said, "Let's go upstairs." I wasn't so sure that was a good idea. I had never been up there before. But the others whispered, "Come on, let's go," and started up. So up we went.

High school classes were in session, and the halls were empty. We walked quickly and quietly, zipping past open doorways to avoid being seen.   In less than a minute we advanced from one end of the hall to the other. No one saw us—luck was running with us. When we reached the stairs at the end of the hall, we started down toward the safety of the first floor. Half way down the stairway turned, and the bottom half of the stairs opened to the first floor hallway. We made the turn, bounding down the steps, and then looked out. And there was Mrs. Sturmire, thirty feet away, leading the fourth grade parade directly at us! Mrs. Sturmire, the screamer ... We were in full view, descending toward her and the parade. Every kid saw us scampering down the stairs, and Mrs. Sturmire recognized us at once.

"What are you doing?! Stop!" came her shout. The four of us hit the first floor and quickly veered left, away from Mrs. Sturmire, breaking toward fourth grade. She shouted again, "STOP!"

A couple guys stopped. I didn't—I kept fleeing, almost in a daze. I thought, "Maybe if I just keep going, somehow it'll be OK...."

"Stop!" she shouted once more. I slowed down.

"I said STOP!" she shouted after me.

I took another step, but realized it was over, finished. I stopped and turned about to meet reality.   Facing me was a hall full of forty or fifty fourth graders, filling the corridor and pressed together, all of them stretching their necks to see what was going on ... to see who was gonna get it.   Mrs. Sturmire stood in front of them, fuming. And next were the four of us, spaced out along the hall where our respective escapes had been cut short.

"Get BACK here!" Mrs. Sturmire screamed at us, pointing to the floor in front of her.

We walked slowly back to her. I was the last one to get there. We formed a lineup, four across, shoulder to shoulder facing her. Mike was at one end; I was on the other. She glared at us.

"What were you doing!?" she shouted.

We told her about being late with our trash and Mrs. Carlemagno's sending us to the cafeteria.

"So why were you on the second floor? You know you're not supposed to be there!"

None of us had an answer. That seemed to make her angrier.

"HOW MANY TIMES have we told you not to go upstairs?! What is WRONG with you?!" she screamed in our faces. The four of us cowered. Our cafeteria classmates were getting a real show.

"You make me so ANGRY!" she shouted, as if our going upstairs was somehow a huge insult aimed personally at her. Then more anger seemed to well up inside her, gushing out of nowhere.

Suddenly she reached for us, putting her left hand on the side of Mike's head and her right on mine. Before I could think, she quick drew her arms in and bonked our four heads together! My head clunked sideways, and I stumbled for a split second as my head bonked off Jack's and bounced backward. I felt like I was in a Three Stooges routine. The class looked on in wonderment as the four of us wobbled about, trying to straighten our heads upright. We must have looked ridiculous. My head didn't hurt, but my pride sure did.

"You NEVER go up there again!" Mrs. Sturmire screamed. "Do you understand?!"

Four bonked heads nodded. We understood. It was crystal clear. No additional shouting was necessary.

"Now, get in line," she ordered. And she marched us at the head of the parade back to fourth grade.

In all my years of schooling since then, I never heard tell of any other head bonk rivaling Mrs. Sturmire's remarkable Quadruple Bonk that day. It was exceptional—delivered with zest, timing and just the right finesse to set all four of us evil doers stumbling about. If they gave awards for that kind of thing, she certainly deserved a big, shiny trophy of some sort. Today, of course, Mrs. Sturmire and the school system would probably be sued by overprotective parents for tactics like hers. Happily, my friends and I somehow managed to walk away from that bonking unscathed—each with his intricate framework of fourth grade multiplication tables still mentally intact.

All in all, I didn't like being on the receiving end of a teacher's anger. But I have to admit Mrs. Sturmire was an excellent communicator and merited superior marks for disciplinary creativity.

Certain Death

So by fourth grade I had come to understand a few things about getting into trouble. There was the kind of trouble that finds you-- my ears-plugged mathematics trouble. In that kind of trouble you weren't trying to do anything wrong, but trouble just sneaked up on you ... and pounced out of nowhere. Like THAT, you were smack in trouble before you even knew what hit.

And there was the kind of trouble where you did the finding— Mrs. Sturmire's bonking. Here you knew you shouldn't choose a certain path, but you considered the choices, understood the risk, and decided to take your chances, mindful a bad outcome might result.

And finally, there was a third kind of trouble—the worst kind. This broke open when the first two kinds of trouble collided, got all jumbled together, events careened out of control and there was no telling what might happen. This strain of trouble could be fatal.

One afternoon I was playing baseball down the street with Bobby. We were taking turns hitting each other flies and grounders across his back yard. His mom wasn't home, so one of Bobby's older brothers and the big kid from next door came out back to pick on us--they liked to give us a hard time. At first they just eased into it, pushing us around a little, disrupting our play, tripping us now and then, and twisting our arms. But after about twenty minutes they got down to the real stuff, wrestling Bobby and me to the ground, sitting on top of us, and bending us in painful headlocks and half nelsons. When I managed to squirm free, I ran off to the safety of one side of the yard and stood there.

Then the two of them ganged up on Bobby and tied him to a tree. When he was bound up, they started twisting the rope around his arms to hurt him even more. As they worked over Bobby, they occasionally turned to me and yelled and threatened—I didn't run off, but I stood at the edge of the yard with my ball bat. They twisted the rope around Bobby's arms a second and third time, and each time I watched the pain seize his face—it really hurt him!

For Bobby's brother, roughing up his little brother was just a routine family sport. But that big neighbor kid really delighted in the pain—he was just plain mean. That kid scared me. But as I stood there, I began to think, "If that kid hurts Bobby one more time, I'm going to hit him with this bat."

Of course, I knew you weren't supposed to hit someone with a weapon like a baseball bat. But this was serious. Bobby was being terrorized and tortured—somehow I had to try to help him. Then the mean kid walked up to Bobby and squeezed the rope again, and I made up my mind. I was going to get him. I quick came up with a plan—I'd whack him in the shin and take off fast—I'd have a head start and his leg would hurt like heck and keep him from coming after me. I thought something like that should work.

I began walking slowly in his direction—a nice and easy walk so he wouldn't suspect anything. The kid eased up on the rope around Bobby and stepped back from the tree. Now he wasn't far off. I calmly approached him, my bat lowered in my right hand. I didn't say a word--I intended to hurt him bad.

The kid turned and saw me close by, but he didn't react to a little twerp like me slowly walking toward him. He just stood there--he had no idea what was coming. When I got almost beside him, all at once I quick raised up the bat and cracked it down hard across his shin bone.

He screamed, and I took off clutching my bat. I had a few seconds head start. He howled at me, but I was running hard and didn't look back. Then he came cursing and cussing after me. Out the driveway--I could hear him running and limping and swearing! "You little son of a bitch!!!!" He was going to kill me! I ran harder! His footsteps got closer and I could hear him panting--his rage was surging right behind me. Fear grabbed at me! I hit the street and veered toward home, racing like never before! Down the street he ran and limped and hobbled in pursuit. I kept running. He strained and stretched, but his anger couldn't quite reach me—I was too fast and his pain was too much. Then I heard his footsteps slow and gradually limp to a stop. I kept running and running, leaving him behind. And he yelled one last curse at me as I streaked off toward home.

Five minutes later when Mom returned with me to the scene of my terror, the situation had completely changed. Bobby was standing in the yard; they had untied him from the tree. He was OK, and his brother and the mean kid were long gone.

As I looked across the yard, all the pain and terror that filled the place a few minutes before—my brush with death--had strangely melted away and vanished. The mean kid was gone, now Mom was in charge, and the world was surprisingly calm, like nothing had ever happened.

V.

From within, just below our surface, another force aspires upward. It doesn't rift and heave at our mass—it's gentle. It animates, fragile but pervasive, like the stirrings of spring in an April woods. It moves to sprout, gain hold in a crevice, to take root and flourish, to find light and decorate the landforms. If it thrives, it will color and cover emerging hills and valleys in a complex majesty, sheltering and sustaining our being, cradling our becoming.

Trees

Life was better in a tree. Up there, resting on a limb, no one bothered you. Above twenty feet, most people didn't even know you were around.

The world was different up high. There you could peer out through the branches, survey your surroundings, get the big picture and see what was going on. The higher you went, the better it got. In Disney's Comics and Stories, whenever Mickey and Goofy were caught up in an adventure and lost in the woods, they'd climb the highest tree to get their bearings and help them decide what to do next. A view from on high could put things in perspective.

Some trees were better to climb than others. Small willows with little, bent-sideways, meandering trunks were OK, but the trunks of bigger ones didn't have enough limbs to work with. And willow wood was soft—even thick branches could give way and crack. Wild cherry trees were pretty good--spacing of the branches gave you plenty to work with, and the wood was strong. In early summer the hard, green cherries were perfect for pea shooters—in a wild cherry you never ran out of ammo. But the bark on cherry branches was smooth and paper-thin, and it scraped off easy, exposing a slippery green layer underneath. So you had to be careful not to let your feet slip in cherry trees. Beech trees were also pretty good— for carving initials, beech bark was best. But really big beech trees grew branches so massive it was difficult to pull yourself around them on the way up.

Some trees just weren't for climbing. Sharp thorns made locust trees impossible. Shagbark hickories weren't for climbing, either. Instead you memorized their locations so you could come back in October and gather the fallen nuts. Large American elms lacked low branches, so you had to pull and shinny your way high up the trunk to the first solid branch. But furrowed elm bark broke away under that scraping and left your arms and clothes covered with gritty, sooty black marks after a climb—elms weren't worth it.

Sugar maples were best. No matter the size of the tree, maples always seemed to have a branch coming out of the trunk right about where you needed one to pull yourself up and another branch to stand on. The branches were big enough to be strong, but small enough not to block your climb. The bark was smooth and almost clean, and the wood wouldn't break on you—you could bend those branches halfway around before they'd splinter. You could trust a sugar maple.

In times of danger, a climbing tree could come in handy. Everybody knew the story of Smokey the Bear, the cub that survived a forest fire out West by climbing a tree. His bear instincts made him scramble high up a tree to escape danger. Kid instincts worked much the same.

One summer day Bobby, Richy and I were sitting in my yard by the driveway. Beside us was a big tin washtub. We had spent the morning prying up rocks in the creek, catching crayfish. We corralled our crayfish into the tub, filled the bottom of the washtub with a couple inches of water from the hose, and added handfuls of stones and rocks to make the crayfish feel at home. Now we were looking for something else to do, and our conversation was following a routine summer vacation pattern.

"What do you want to do?" Richy asked the two of us.

I nudged a gray crayfish with a stick, trying to get him to move. "I don't know. What do you want to do?"

"Oh ... I don't know," Richy answered.

"Do you want to go catch more crayfish?" I asked.

"No, not really," Richy replied.

My crayfish didn't want to move, so I poked at him again.

Bobby was tossing pebbles into the gravel driveway. He spoke up. "Do you want to go watch them work on the house?" A new house was going up on Meadowview, a few empty lots up the hill from my house. The foundation was dug, and they'd probably be pouring concrete.

"That'd be OK," Richy answered. His dad had a concrete business, and Richy was interested in building.

I thought about Bobby's house suggestion. It was something to do. I put my stick down. "Yeah, sure, that's fine with me," I said.

We got up and started walking. A row of wild cherry trees extended from my yard up the little hill, through a field along the backside of the empty lots. At one time a wire fence had followed the tree line. We walked under the trees to the top of the slope. From there we could see out across the small field toward the construction, about forty yards away. A concrete truck was on the property.

"Hey, wait a second," Bobby said, and he stopped. Richy and I looked at him. "I was just thinking," Bobby continued. "Let's write our names in the cement."

"No way ... They won't let us do that," I said. Workmen would let you watch from nearby, but they always made you stay away from the work.

"Well, we could sneak up, and do it when they're not looking," Bobby answered. With two older brothers, Bobby was much farther along on the learning curve than Richy and me. "Come on," he encouraged. Richy and I weren't so sure.

We talked about it under the trees, and Bobby pushed his idea. Richy and I weren't as bold as Bobby, but gradually we came around, and a plan took shape. We would crawl through the field toward the site. The weeds in the field were three or four feet tall, and dense so no one would see us. We'd go toward the back corner of the foundation, where we could hide behind some dirt piles. Then, from behind the piles we'd crawl close enough to write our names when no one was looking. We all agreed, and we got down low and started forward.

It was easy to sneak through the weeds without being spotted— only a few field crickets and lady bugs noticed our passing. When we came to the edge of the field near the dirt piles, we paused. There were several workmen busy laying concrete at the far side of the site. In the back corner of the site, closest to us, there was a smooth, fresh pour of cement—that part of our plan seemed perfect. But the dirt piles were smaller than we expected—they weren't going to conceal us nearly as well as we figured. And from our new forward observation post, the workmen now looked awfully close.

I whispered to the others, "I don't think we can do this—they're going to see us."

Richy saw things the same way, but Bobby wanted to press on. We were only about fifteen feet from the cement.

"Well … why don't you go ahead, then," I said to Bobby. "We'll stay here."

Richy and I lay low in the weeds and watched Bobby crawl forward. He had a small stick in one hand for writing. He reached the dirt piles and paused, peering across at the workers. He waited a couple minutes, and when they all looked busy, he squirmed forward on his stomach, up to the fresh cement. Richy and I watched from the weeds as the workers shoveled and smoothed on the far side and Bobby began etching away with his stick.

It took him about a half minute to write, then he pulled back his arm and started to push away from the foundation.

"Hey!" someone shouted … then louder—"Hey! You!"

A man was looking across the site at Bobby.

"You … what are you doing there!" he yelled.

This wasn't part of our plan. Bobby sprang up and took off toward Richy and me. He shot by us, and we stumbled to our feet and fled after him. More shouts … "You kids! Come here!"

We raced downhill through the field, sending bugs and grasshoppers scattering in our wake. We reached the far edge of the field where the men couldn't see us anymore, and we kept running. When we got to the trees we slowed a second to catch our breath, then our kid instincts kicked in. In a clump of wild cherries, each of us found a big trunk and started climbing. Up we went toward safety—they wouldn't find us here. We climbed quickly to twenty or thirty feet, and then we stopped, braced against some high branches in silence. And we waited, looking back and forth at each other through the leaves, trusting we were safe and that nothing more would happen.

After a couple minutes of hiding quietly in the trees, it looked like we might be OK. But then we heard someone coming. Down below, one of the workmen was walking along the tree line, coming our way. He was looking all around as he moved, studying the weeds and trees, taking slow steps. As he approached nearer, he spotted one of us, then the other two. There was nothing we could do—we were trapped. He came closer, staring up at the three of us. Finally, underneath us, he stopped walking. It was over.

He called up. "Which one of you is Bobby Aggleman?"

The man didn't have Bobby's last name quite right. But for Richy and me, another kid instinct kicked in and we weren't going to quibble over spelling. In unison Richy and I pointed at Bobby—"He is!" There was no "All for one and one for all" stuff--Richy and I knew when our necks were on the line. And Bobby stared across at Richy and me, giving the two of us a well-deserved dirty look.

"You boys come on down," the man said.

When we reached the ground, the workman made Bobby go back up to the house with him and smooth out his name. Richy and I stayed behind and waited under the trees.

Tree instincts didn't always work out. Even so, sometimes you could trust a tree more than your friends.

One summer my neighbor Fred and I took up tree swinging. Tree swinging was a Midwest version of Tarzan, using sugar maples instead of vines. First you'd find a good-sized maple in the woods— not a broad round one like you'd find in an open yard or field, but a tall, slender one stretching up through adjacent foliage, seeking sunlight. Then you'd climb almost to the top, where the main trunk narrowed to about four inches. Then you would grab on tight and lean one way and then back the other, trying to sway the tree from side to side. You'd keep swaying it more and more, farther and farther out, until you could finally reach over and grab the branches of an adjacent tree. Then you'd pull the two trees together, cross from your tree to the other, and climb back down the second tree

70

to the ground. The way maples bent, tree swinging worked best about thirty or forty feet up.

Neither Fred nor I broke any bones that summer.

Dad ran his air conditioning business out of his green panel truck. Sometimes in the back of the truck he carted home good pieces of discarded lumber picked up at job sites during the day. One summer Dad gave me the wood and nails I needed to build a small tree platform--a couple short two-by-four's for support and a few ¾ inch boards for the platform. I built it across two parallel limbs in a tree by the driveway. It was a comfortable little space--about three feet square and six feet off the ground. But it was out in the open for all to see. So the next year I built another platform between a maple and an elm out front. This one was a little bigger, about seven feet up and more concealed behind tree trunks and branches. It was a good place to climb to and sit. But in the middle of the front lawn, there was only so much you could do up there in that tight space. Something more was needed.

When we moved to Pleasant Valley, Dad had borrowed a tractor and dug out the creek in the side yard to form a pond, almost a hundred feet long and fifty feet wide. On the far side of the pond, a willow with a giant trunk had long ago fallen and was growing along the ground. But over the years, three big new trunks sprouted and now rose up from the fallen base.   The new trunks and their branches created a broad willow fifty feet tall, towering beside the pond. Each of the trunks was almost two feet thick at the base, and together they formed a broad triangle stretching upward—the perfect location for a tree house.

Dad helped with the first support beams, and after that Richy, Fred, Bobby and I built the house in stages over a couple summers. When completed, perched high amid yellow branches and sheltered within a curtain of willow leaves, the tree house was a masterpiece.

The best feature was the picture window, seven feet long, looking out on the pond. Here we brought the wall up waist high and left a three-foot tall window along the top. One of the supporting trunks came up through the middle, dividing the picture window in half.

Standing at the window, fifteen feet above the water, you could survey the pond for snakes, snapping turtles and schools of baby catfish moving along the shallow edge like a black amoeba. Or you could grab the trunk, climb out the window and twist around onto the roof for an even better view. Two side walls extended from floor to roof, each with a big shuttered window. We rigged up rope pulleys to operate hinged shutters so they could be closed when under attack. The flat roof was constructed of two-by-six's and two-by-eight's—it was the last part of the structure built, and the strongest. The roof could withstand anything and even helped hold the willow trunks together in strong wind. We strategically located narrow openings in side walls for observation and for pea shooters to repel attackers. An eight-foot ladder rose from the ground to the square entrance door on the back wall. Anyone could climb the ladder, but we constructed the door from the hardest oak Dad ever brought home—you could barely pound a big 16 penny spike into it without bending the nail. We anchored our oak door with a couple heavy steel hinges and padlocked it shut every night.

To someone passing by on Pleasant Valley, our tree house probably didn't look like much—some walls of unsightly boards nailed together up a big willow. We never thought about painting it or trying to make it look pretty. In our eyes, it was darn near perfect … a cool place to eat peanut butter and jelly lunch on a July day, shelter from gooey mud balls scooped up from the pond by neighborhood invaders, a spot to watch the kingfisher swoop from his phone line perch across the water, a sharpshooter post for firing BB's at toy boats sailing below, a trusty floor at 2 am sleeping out with friends, and a late afternoon reprieve from having to think about homework on bright fall days. Up there, the world was of your own making—a kids' world measured in kids' dimensions.

Fifth Grade

There were more fifth graders in Canfield than the school building could hold. To solve the problem, two 5th grade classes--including Mrs. Reilly's--were moved to the basement of the Presbyterian Church on Main Street at the corner of Wadsworth, a half block from school. So each day Mrs. Reilly led the class along the sidewalk, back and forth between our church classroom and the buses and cafeteria at the main school building.

No sidewalks existed on Palmyra or Pleasant Valley. Roadsides in the country were bordered with loose gravel and a foot or two of weeds sloping to a muddy drainage ditch. But in the village, sidewalks led everywhere. Most were sandy brown concrete, while older streets had big, blackened rectangular slabs of stone laid end-to-end. Walking along, you had to watch your step under old trees where roots had lifted the slabs, so you didn't trip on the edges.

Traveling through town on the school bus or in a car, you were confined--all you could do was look out at the houses and parts of the village as you passed. But walking along a sidewalk was a different way of traveling. On sidewalks you weren't just looking out as you passed. A sidewalk seemed a part of town, part of each front yard and house it touched. You drove down a village street to get somewhere else; sidewalks seemed to invite you in.

So each day Larry and Ron, Nancy and Patricia, Jeff, Lela, Dave and the rest of Mrs. Reilly's fifth grade class journeyed back and forth, shuffling through a fall cover of crispy red maple leaves, pressing fresh boot prints into a new blanket of snow, and passing tufts of spring daffodils bordering tidy lawns. And as we walked, our little fifth grade band merged with the village, meeting and visiting a few moments each home we touched.

I liked living in the country. But I also envied kids who lived in town and could travel the sidewalks to school.

I must have gotten most of that mischief out of my system in fourth grade. For by fifth grade all those previous years of schooling—listening, paying attention, following instructions--seem to have taken hold.

Doing well at school had become the goal. With each star on a writing paper, OK on a history quiz and A- on another arithmetic test, the goal was reinforced. I wasn't smart enough to see how the process worked in a big circle—the expectation of doing well prompted effort to learn, which resulted in good marks which further increased expectations. So by fifth grade I had somehow

73

made my choices about school—like most others I had fallen into line. I wasn't particularly curious about how the world worked—I didn't wonder much about things. I was just motivated to do well and get good grades.

Aside from comic books, reading didn't interest me. I read what I needed for book reports and studied assigned material in text books. But given a choice between reading and doing something, I chose the doing.

By fifth grade, I thought we were too old for a teacher to read us stories. But Mrs. Reilly thought otherwise. Every day after lunch, when we came inside from recess in the parking area behind the church, Mrs. Reilly would open a book and read for fifteen minutes to settle us down for the afternoon. Somewhere she had come across a series of adventure stories about a group of British kids our age. So each day after recess, the characters Philip, Jack and Lucy-Ann took center stage in Mrs. Reilly's classroom, as they encountered mystery and danger in The River of Adventure and The Castle of Adventure. The day Mrs. Reilly read the tale of those kids crawling through narrow tunnels in the copper mines on The Island of Adventure was the first time a story ever emerged from ink and paper and became real. It turned out that reading an adventure story could be a little like traveling a sidewalk and stepping into new places.

It was a breakthrough for me—of sorts. After that, I sometimes picked up a book to read. Even so, it was generally just a Hardy Boys story, and usually only when I was sick and Mom was making me stay home in bed for the day.

Whistles

It was a long way from Pleasant Valley to the nearest railroad tracks. Five miles to the northeast, stretched along the Mahoning River, the busy tracks of the B&O, the Pittsburgh & Lake Erie, the Erie, and the Pennsylvania Railroad weaved mile after mile through the steel mill complex of Struthers, Campbell, Youngstown and Brier Hill. Those railroads produced an incessant ringing of train whistles

74

and horns, rumbles of thuds and thunders of every kind. But at five miles away, meshed in the din of the steel mills, and muffled behind the noises of thousands of homes, businesses and city streets covering the South Side, no sounds from those railroads could ever have penetrated all the way to Pleasant Valley. But on rare occasions, one did.

It would happen only every now and then, at night, when calm had settled over the countryside. I'd be out in the yard, and it would come suddenly. Beneath the stillness of the evening and the strain of the crickets, I would sense low throbbing of diesels far off, working hard … reverberating through the darkness. Over a few seconds the sound would grow louder, clearer, rise up, last a short minute, and then vanish as quickly as it had materialized. The throbbing was unmistakable, deep and full—sometimes I could almost feel it, that pounding of those far off diesel locomotives. One night when I was sleeping in the tree house, the throbbing rose up so strong it sounded almost as if the locomotive was coming down the street. I was certain—the sound was a train.

As my knowledge of trains around Youngstown grew, I came to piece together an explanation for the sound. The noise always came from exactly the same direction, a single distant point. I guessed it was the Market Street Bridge in Youngstown. The bridge began at the top of a steep hill along a bend of the Mahoning River. The bridge carried Market from the hillside above the river downward to the valley floor, over railroads and river, ending two blocks from the square in downtown Youngstown. From south to north, the long bridge spanned first the two tracks of the Lake Erie & Eastern, then the B&O tracks curving along the river, next the river, then the Pennsylvania tracks on the north bank, the B&O freight house, and finally skimmed the rooftops of Republic Steel before landing in the city square. The drop from the rim of the hill to the river must have been a hundred feet.

Westbound trains on the B&O had to stop at Center Street crossing, a mile east of the bridge, in the shadow of Republic Steel blast furnaces. After they cleared Center Street, the engines would strain to get the train moving again up to mainline speed. There was nothing polite about those diesels—pulling against a long freight train they spewed exhaust with booming vengeance. So when a B&O freight pounded into that curve under the bridge, the bend in the hillside formed a kind of echo chamber. I figured that the chamber somehow concentrated the sound of the engines and flung it skyward. And if the stillness in the air was just right, that's when I could hear it. As soon as the engines rounded the curve and left the echo chamber, the sound disappeared, returning the night to the crickets.

I never knew if my explanation of the source of that distant train sound was correct. But it seemed logical on those charmed evenings when the stray echo of a far off train took hold and rolled out across the land.

I heard only one other train on Pleasant Valley.

A big wild cherry tree grew along the driveway in front of our house. After we moved in, Dad climbed to the top of the tree and attached a spotlight at the end of a thick electric cord. He draped the cord through the high branches and connected it to the house wiring, so you could turn the light on from a hallway switch. The spotlight hung downward, illuminating part of the driveway and a patch of yard beneath the tree.

On snowy nights, Carol, Nancy and I would turn on the light to see how thick the flakes were falling and check the progress of the storm—maybe a snow day tomorrow? One winter evening I bundled up in boots and gray hood and went outside to check the storm. Snow had been coming down for several hours, and we had about nine inches on the ground. The forecast on the six o'clock news had been promising--with another six inches, there was a good chance school would be cancelled in the morning. Standing under the spotlight, I gazed up at the flakes spilling out of the darkness and filling the light around me. It was a frigid, icy snow. The flakes were sharp, and they glistened as they fell through the light. The snow was coming hard, and there was little wind, so the flakes glided quietly.

Then I heard the train whistle, off to the east. It was an unusual high-pitched tone--two longs floating into the light. At first I questioned the sound. But the two longs were followed by a short and another long chime. It was as clear as day.   From that direction, it had to be the Youngstown & Southern, a little short line railroad that ran through Boardman.   The whistle pattern meant that he was probably blowing for one of the many crossings along the stretch of track by Southern Avenue.   Somewhere I had learned that when the Y&S dieselized, they took whistles from their steam engines before scrapping and put them on the new diesels.   The sound of those old steam whistles was unique.

I turned toward the whistle.   There were other crossings along Southern Avenue he would pass in a few minutes.   So I breathed as quietly as I could and focused all my senses into the darkness, hoping to hear it blow for the next crossing.   Flakes continued to fall, and icy crystals sparkled under the light.   Minutes passed, but no whistle.   I walked from under the spotlight into the darkness of the front yard, and listened again....   Long minutes passed, more waiting and listening.... But there was only the snow. After twenty minutes of straining and searching, it was getting late.   So I kicked aside the deepening snow, crossed back into the spotlight and went inside. I never heard that train again.

It didn't make sense why I heard that lone Y&S whistle that night. Clouds laden with snow and falling flakes normally obscure sound and muffle far off noise.   Rather, winter sounds carry farthest on calm, bitter, cloudless nights, when the snow crunches tight underfoot, cold seems to purify the still air, bare branches scratch against a forever sky, and stars glare down.

But that night something uncommon happened, and the vibrations from a distant little train landed softly on the snows of my front yard.

Big Woods

The woods around Pleasant Valley offered plenty of adventure. But around fifth or sixth grade some of us from the neighborhood began visiting the big woods on the far side of Raccoon Road.

You approached this woods by hiking up Meadowview past the ball field, then along Raccoon Road, cutting away from the road and entering the horse pasture near Thompson Lane. The two or three horses grazing near the old wooden barn in the center of the pasture normally didn't bother you, but you had to be careful—

77

once a startled horse charged out of the barn and almost ran over Bobby. But we kept going. Beyond the horses, you crossed another fence and entered a second large, open field. You proceeded across that field to the distant fence line, where you finally stood at the edge of the woods.

This woods was much larger than the tracts along Pleasant Valley. It spread miles across the top of a broad, low ridge. An upland woods, it lacked streams with their stands of willows, pockets of cattails, big beeches and sycamores. Here the woodland was flat, heavily forested and open under hardwood oaks and hickories. A thick layer of brown, matted leaves, rotting into the soil and covering forest floor made for an easy walk. But the land lacked defined paths and reference points to help you mark your way. So you wandered. Openness amid the trees and the unexplored vastness of the woods drew you in. We never ventured deep enough to emerge at the other side.

When I went into the big woods with Bobby or Fred, usually we would probe along under the high treetops without chancing upon anything unusual. But one summer day as we explored, the trees parted, the forest uncovered and we stood at the edge of an opening in the woods dominated by a mass of grapevines. The vines had overgrown a grove of small trees, draping them with a bright green blanket of grape leaves. The blanket covered the grove, forming a mound sixty feet wide extending way up, overtopping even the highest branches. The smooth surface was supported by the thick mass of vines hidden underneath and anchored to the tree trunks. The growth rustled in the breeze and the trunks slow creaked like billowing sails pulling against masts of a tall ship. Of course we had to climb the smooth contours to the tops of the trees—like climbing pirate ship rigging to the crow's-nest. Later we hoisted big branches gathered from the surrounding woods and constructed a hidden platform up within the grape canopy--a little wooden nest. Under a bright blue sky, we rested on the platform and gazed out on our great green ship at sail in the forest.

The summer forest might welcome you, but in winter the forest changed. The trees no longer offered shelter, the expanse of the woods seemed to broaden, and the thought of numbing cold filling the forest caused you to pause before venturing in. During summer you might enter the forest on a lark. Come winter, a trek into the woods was not to be taken lightly.

One Thanksgiving morning I awoke to fresh snow. A few inches covered the ground, and flakes were falling at a good clip. The temperature hung in the 20's with light winds moving down from the northwest. After breakfast, I decided to go for a walk in the woods. Mom was in the kitchen mixing chopped celery and dried bread for stuffing. She said OK, as long as I got back in time for turkey. So I went to the basement and suited up with long underwear and jeans, two pairs of wool socks under my tall brown boots. I added T shirt, flannel shirt and sweat shirt under a gray hood, then stocking hat and leather gloves—I was ready. I opened the door, and off I went into the quiet countryside, trudging through the falling snow, leaving a long trail of footprints, heading up Meadowview toward the big woods. It was a perfect day for a walk.

Up to Raccoon and along snowy tire tracks, into the horse field, through the fence, then deeper into the falling snow and across the next open expanse to the edge of the forest…. There I entered the big woods.

One of my favorite TV shows was Hawkeye and the Last of the Mohicans. Hawkeye and his old Indian partner Chingachkook trod the vast forests which covered the Northeast, some two hundred years before. In the black and white television tales, Hawkeye's primal woods was much like mine. I walked and remembered episodes where the frontiersman pushed overland through snowy, stark forests, fighting the cold and ice to reach the warmth of a distant settlement. Worn from travel, he paused in swirling snow amid tall trunks to catch his breath. Then he marched on. He was alone and isolated in his journey through the wilderness.

That morning I imagined I was traveling the same frozen forest. I thought about roast turkey and warm sausage stuffing somewhere ahead in my settlement. And I felt my soft breathing and puffed out frosty air, as I pushed on through the snow. Then I stopped to rest.

Beneath falling snow, the winter woods seemed a holy place. A white stillness hung in the air, broken only by whispers of winds stirring high branches. Flakes drifted down upon the carpet of

79

snow, filling the air with the tinkling of ice crystals, like tiny wind chimes, their clear notes almost too pure to hear. Dark trees and bark, overlapping branches and limbs, struck a composition in black edges and borders cast against white forms and accents. White grew along the black edges and upward upon the undergrowth. As I peered into the crisscross black and white, a layer of contrasts appeared embedded behind the nearest branches, and smaller lines and edges overlay behind that, and still other tiny whites and blacks more distant composed the rest. All the world was simple black and white, but the patterns were far too intricate to grasp. Another soft wind stirred the treetops. I felt at once solitary and surrounded.

That afternoon Mom's turkey and gravy were especially good.

Sixth Grade

Miss Gould knew how to run a classroom—she had been doing it for years. She was tall and thin, blonde hair cut above shoulders. Her tight skirts below the knee and angular frame perched on high heels forced an awkward, exaggerated walk. She was stricter than most, but she always acted with cause—sixth graders had no reason to fear her. I liked her.

The most noteworthy thing about Miss Gould was her artsy, theatrical bent. She moved with a flair for the dramatic and observed with a critical, artful eye. Other teachers didn't share that style. So Miss Gould sometimes seemed a bit out of place in the school system--out of her element. After all, Canfield was a plain place, mostly farms and fields, Midwest practical. Theatrics didn't loom large in Canfield. In Canfield you didn't speak for effect—you opened your mouth because you had something to say—no more, no less. Regardless of her fit, Miss Gould knew her profession and carried herself well—not the least bashful expressing that special bent.

By sixth grade I had come to recognize there were usually one or two students in every classroom who could draw well—like Patricia or Bonnie--who had talent for capturing images and forms on paper. Not me--I couldn't draw worth beans. After mastering stick figures, square houses, green puffy trees and round yellow suns in first grade, then squarish, awkward body forms later in elementary school, by fourth and fifth grade my artwork gravitated to panoramic battle scenes. Sometimes I created lines of Union cannon on the left side of the paper hurling shot at rows of Confederate cannon arrayed along the right side. Or I drew World War II naval battles, with fleets of battleships, cruisers and carriers under attack from formations of tiny fighters and bombers dropping from the skies. After setting each battle scene and aiming all the guns, I would then trace out trajectories of the cannon balls and machine gun fire and bombs, adding explosion after explosion to my depiction wherever the fire hit ship or aircraft. That was my inspired art.

One week the class was studying ancient Persia, the Fertile Crescent between the Tigris and Euphrates Rivers. For that week's art project Miss Gould instructed us to draw something related to our history lesson. I had found a picture of a Persian soldier, complete with helmet, sword, boots, heavy leather and metal outfit, and had spent a couple days working in pencil to recreate him on my paper. And for the first time in my drawing career, I was actually succeeding. I had his arms and shoulders proportioned right, and his detailed helmet and raised sword looked good. He held his shield with the other arm, and his body looked almost natural, like he was ready to swing the sword down. He had muscles in his legs where he should--like a real person. His heavy boots covered his calves, and his bent knees made him look ready to fight. "This is pretty good," I thought, admiring my creation ... "Yeah, pretty darn good." I was ready to put down my pencil and switch to crayons to add color. I was eager to hear what Miss Gould would say as she made her rounds to review how each of us was progressing.

When she came to my desk, she bent down and paused. "So, Bob, let's see how you're doing."

I waited for her compliment.

"Let's see now. I think he needs a little help, maybe a little more like this," she said. And she took her big rubber eraser and erased one of his legs and his boot. Then she erased the other, brushed eraser residue aside and sketched in new legs, longer and more flowing.

"Now, let's do this with his arm," she said, and erased his upright arm and sword. She penciled new lines for his arm and elbow, and his new sword was fatter and more curved. It didn't look anything like the solid weapon I had drawn.

"Let's change his helmet a bit," she said. And her eraser rubbed out his head and helmet, and she drew new lines overtop the old. His head became much bigger, and all the detail I had worked into his helmet was gone.

"There, Bob … doesn't that look much better?" she said.

We hadn't yet learned about rhetorical questions in school, but I knew enough to keep my mouth shut. Then she straightened and walked to the next desk.

I looked at my picture. Almost all of my original lines were gone. The image was completely transformed—that soldier didn't look anything like he did before. Miss Gould had obliterated my fighter and inserted some stylized imposture in his place! She might as well have taken my picture, torn it up and thrown it away. I was as angry as I was surprised. The best thing I ever drew was ruined! "What was so wrong with my picture?" I thought. I looked again at the new image and wondered, "How come her drawing is so much better?"

In arithmetic, there was always a right answer, and if you worked at the problem hard enough, you could figure it out. But art was not like arithmetic—for me it was a mystery, like wandering a no man's land in the fog. I guessed there must be some kind of right answer in art, some kind of way to make a picture look so it was correct. But I sure couldn't figure it out.

I worked with the new lines Miss Gould gave me, trying to recreate some of my original, realistic soldier. I thought maybe I could salvage portions of him within Miss Gould's new forms. But her shapes were completely different--too stylish and fancy. After a little trying I gave up--he was gone. So I colored in the lines and turned in the project.

Map reading was an important part of sixth grade. It was important to know where you were and where the rest of the world was. Mounted above the blackboard in front of the classroom was a rolled up world map. It was about five feet across, and you could pull it down to view, like you'd pull down a window shade. One day Miss Gould called on Jimmy to go to the map and trace out the route Marco Polo had followed from Italy to the Far East. We had been studying the journeys of Marco Polo the last couple of days, and Miss Gould expected Jimmy to know the route.

Jimmy lived on his family's farm a couple miles west of town. When Jimmy and I were younger, I once visited his farm to play, and I was impressed with how Jimmy crawled through the hay bale tunnels his big brothers had constructed in the hayloft of their barn. Jimmy easily knew his way through the close, dark tunnels, along the musty twists and turns of the stacked hay bales. But finding his way across that sprawling world map was a different story.

Jimmy walked to the front of the room and stood beside Europe. He was short for his age, and Miss Gould towered over him. "All right, Jimmy, show the class the route."

He found Italy, and knew enough to start tracing a journey eastward from there toward Asia. But once he got beyond the Mediterranean Sea, he had no idea where Marco went. Jimmy paused, then fidgeted a moment, then slid his hand down toward the Indian Ocean. "No, Jimmy, that's not the way he went. Remember, he went overland during the trip to China. Start again."

So Jimmy retraced the journey back to the Mediterranean and tried again. He studied the map, trying to recall something—anything--about the route. He should have known the way. The longer he paused, the more irritated Miss Gould grew. Everyone in class could see it building.

"How did he cross the Near East?" she prodded. Jimmy hesitated, and then his hand started wandering north into Russia. "No! That's not right. Marco Polo didn't go up there," she interrupted. "First he went to Bagdad," and she stretched a long arm out and pointed over Jimmy at Bagdad. Little Jimmy stood there. "Didn't you study your homework last night?" Her tone was sharp and accusing. "You should know this material!" she glared. The room was still.

Just then the classroom door opened, and in walked Mr. Johnson, the Superintendent of Canfield Public Schools. A classroom visit from the Superintendent was a rare event. He paused politely near the door, to temper his interruption and allow Miss Gould to continue. When she saw him, an instant transformation occurred.

Miss Gould smiled a bright, cheerful greeting, "Well hello, Mr. Johnson! It's good to see you." Her irritation with Jimmy had vanished. "We were just reviewing Marco Polo's journey here at the map."

"That's fine," Mr. Johnson offered. "Why don't you go ahead and finish, Miss Gould."

Without missing a beat, Miss Gould smiled down at Jimmy and in sweet tones continued. "Now, Jimmy, after Marco Polo left the Mediterranean Sea, recall how he entered the Near East, traveling first to Bagdad." And she took Jimmy's hand, raised it to the map, and gently guided his course through the Near East and Persia. "And then he went north of India into the western part of China," and she smiled across at Mr. Johnson as she carefully moved Jimmy's outstretched arm across the map. Jimmy didn't know what hit him, and the rest of the class sat mum, transfixed at the spectacle. When Miss Gould and Jimmy finally reached Peking, she released his hand. "You may go back to your seat now, Jimmy."

Jimmy walked back to his desk, relieved and now grinning wide at his good fortune, and Mr. Johnson walked over to Miss Gould. The two conversed quietly, while Ralph and Danny and Jane and Chris and the rest of us kids strained to hear what was going on. But the adults spoke too softly to hear. After a minute, they smiled at each other, nodded, and Mr. Johnson left.

We never learned what Mr. Johnson's visit was all about. Nothing changed in the weeks that followed, and our daily sixth grade routine with Miss Gould continued to unfold as before. I never mentioned it to anyone, but I was embarrassed for Miss Gould that day--that she felt compelled to act like that for her boss, knowing her little students were looking on, surely critiquing her performance. I imagine she had her reasons. But still, I bet it hurt.

As the year progressed, we continued to study our explorer maps, following Columbus to the New World, the voyage of Magellan around the globe and Henry Hudson's search for the Northwest Passage. But on that day when Mr. Johnson came to sixth grade, Miss Gould taught the class a valuable lesson in understanding landscapes in the workaday world. Certainly it's important to know where you want to go and how to get there. But sometimes it's also important to understand your little place in the world and what you might have to do to remain there.

There was one occasion each school year when Miss Gould came into her own--a brief time when she wasn't out of her element, when her flair for the dramatic could rise up and sing. Every year fifth and sixth grades collaborated on a musical, an operetta, directed by the school music teacher. The performance was a major event on the school calendar. Weeks in advance, everyone in the two grades began practicing chorus songs, a cast was chosen, mimeograph machines spit out copies of the long script, lines were memorized and solos rehearsed. Fifth and sixth grade teachers worked on stage sets, and proud moms cut and sewed and prepared costumes for their budding actors and actresses. In the week leading up to the big Friday and Saturday night performances, fifth and sixth grade classrooms adjourned from regular lessons to the high school auditorium to put finishing touches on the show. Several hundred parents, students and Canfield theater goers would attend each performance. And throughout the process Miss Gould was a steady presence--at home behind the scenes, standing close beside the music teacher listening, helping to organize the effort, coaching lines, advising, making scenery and props, and lending her critical eye and ear to the production.

In fifth grade the school performed Tom Sawyer. I played one of Tom's friends and had a couple lines. Being in the play was OK. But I was more struck by all that was necessary for a big production to come together and surprised by what a bunch of lowly fifth and sixth graders could actually accomplish.

In sixth grade, the music teacher announced we would perform the Wizard of Oz, complete with ruby slippers, a bevy of munchkins, choruses of Over the Rainbow, witches and yellow brick roads. I was picked to be the scarecrow--I suppose because I could memorize lines and didn't freeze up in front of an audience. Though I wasn't a good singer, I was a good enough singer—anyone seated in the back of the auditorium could hear me, and I could

85

generally carry a tune. I didn't like having to sing solo, but I liked the scarecrow part.

The weeks leading up to the gala were busier than I had known. After-school practices replaced bus rides home. Each line had to be exact, and Miss Gould ensured that inflection was just so. You learned to smile, to gesture at the right time, and to follow the prescribed movements about the stage. When to speak, where to go, where to stand, how to move your arms…. It was a lot to remember. Mom made a colorful scarecrow costume, blue jeans and light blue checkered shirt, bright red and yellow patches sewn here and there, and a big straw hat accented with loose tuffs of hay poking out at my wrists and pockets. Evenings before bed, I practiced my lines over and over—the sour odor of blue mimeograph ink was a constant companion.

Friday came, and everyone backstage was all nerves. But at the appointed hour the auditorium lights dimmed, the audience became still, the curtain rose and the operetta began. My sixth grade classmate Nancy played Dorothy. She was a much better singer than I was, and carried the story and songs through the first scenes from Kansas to Oz. When the curtain rose on my first scene along the yellow brick road, and the force of those stage lights and spotlights hit, it knocked me hard. But all that practicing somehow automatically kicked in, and once I got through my "If I Only Had a Brain" solo, and Dorothy and I started down the yellow brick road, I wasn't scared any more. I could look down from the stage into that bright glare and the blur of heads in the dark audience, and I was fine—I knew what I was supposed to do and was pretty sure I could get through it.

Bill played the Tin Man. His robot costume was fashioned of heavy cardboard painted gray. His outfit was realistic, but the edges of the cardboard dug into his arms and legs and hurt him. Between acts, teachers worked backstage to trim the cardboard and ease his pain. Glen was our Cowardly Lion, and Wicked Witch Carol and Good Witch Lela waved their wands and cast their spells as our journey through Oz progressed. Ken played the Wizard, and Richy from Meadowview was the Emerald City guard. Richy wore a bright green uniform, with lots of gold trim and a tall green hat—he looked like a drum major in a band. That night we fifth and sixth graders formed an odd assortment of costumed, painted up kids.

Dorothy, the Tin Man, the Lion and I came to the Emerald City gate twice during the play—the first time on our arrival at the City, and the second after we had melted the Wicked Witch and were returning with her ruby slippers. During the Saturday night show, on our first arrival at the City, Richy got his lines crossed up and our dialogue somehow shifted to the second time—just like that we skipped a couple of scenes! When the curtain fell on that Emerald City gate scene, there was mass confusion backstage, as actresses and Munchkins and stagehands scurried around in near panic, trying to decide what to do next. But under Miss Gould's snap backstage direction, we fast forwarded a couple scenes, regrouped, changed scenery and prepared to pick up the advanced story line. Thanks to Miss Gould, somehow we pulled it off fine.

Following the last curtain call, the whole scene was festive. Everyone was all smiles, full of bright energy and congratulations. Relieved teachers, happy kids and proud parents crowded together in laughter. Joyful Munchkins mingled with lions and witches, and classmates teased and poked at each other's costumes. All the work, planning, rehearsing, practicing and nerves had come together that night and found expression. Dads raised cameras, and flashbulbs popped. Our little school community was one in celebration. That evening it seemed Dorothy had it exactly right-- there was no place like home.

Sometimes we do things that seem to matter, to make a difference--things that you just know are really important and shouldn't be forgotten. Not monumental things that change the world—just everyday things. But they're events which somehow should live on, things where you know there ought to be a stone tablet somewhere to chisel that brief, fleeting instant into the ages.

That Wizard of Oz operetta was one of those celebrations. That evening a bunch of kids shared a path into a land beyond. There they found a stiff dose of magic in the glare of stage lights, some truth within the make believe, and a spirit in the production that would help carry them forward. That evening, in some unspoken way, those kids began growing into something more than a simple gathering of children. They began coalescing into a class.

Maybe Miss Gould, with that darn old flair of hers for the dramatic, was on to something after all.

Our dimensions grow, and the terrains we frequent expand. Early swells grow to hills, and the hills lead on to higher ridges. As we move outward, pathways become more difficult. Fissures widen to faults. Gentle streams merge and broaden to wide flows which must be crossed. In the distance, the way forward steepens.

On some slopes the earth is broken and darkened, and we may choose not to go there. Other passages taken may deny return. The next step is unclear, but we're compelled to press on.

Football

I played baseball because I liked it. I played football because I had to.

At first, football was just another sport. As a little kid I liked to throw and kick and catch Dad's worn leather football from the 1930's. That playing, along with a love of running, got me started. So, by fourth or fifth grade, when fall rolled around and a chill worked the air, Richy, Bobby and I would put aside our bats and gloves, pick up a pair of shoulder pads, and convert the Meadowview baseball field to a football field.

On the bus ride home from school we'd round up Danny and Terry from up on Raccoon Road, Ralph and Tom over on Adeer Drive and other guys from beyond the neighborhood to meet at the field. You needed at least three or four guys on each side to have a decent game, so we asked older, bigger kids, too—anyone in bicycle distance. Within twenty minutes of stepping off the bus, players would begin arriving at the field--guys in scruffy blue jeans still dirty from the last game, canvass black tennis shoes, torn jerseys, floppy shoulder pads and wobbly, oversized plastic helmets. We'd pick teams--the big guys usually trying to stack the deck against the little ones--kick off, and begin running and tackling and knocking each other around the local gridiron.

At our field, there were no grandstands packed with screaming parents or cheerleaders, no fans or coaches looking on—only a few disinterested crows peering down from the high trees beyond Kaufel's yard, or an occasional red-winged blackbird calling from a dry milkweed across Raccoon. And there were no goal posts or neat chalk yard lines, no bands and glory, no macho trash talking, or showboating for the TV audience. Ours was a game of basics, of bumps and knocks and bruises, of skinned elbows and twisted ankles, of facing up to that big kid with the ball coming at you, of sprained wrists and sore fingers, of getting dragged down gang tackled one play, then trying to outrun 'em all the next down. And no matter how hard you got knocked to the ground, it was understood that you would get up and do it again next play. Each of us was out there chasing after a football, banging into others chasing the same thing, trying to earn his rightful place on the team. And for some of us, football began to fuse with self respect.

Back and forth across the field we'd go, trampling down the weeds and kicking up the cool earth, shouting for the ball and bracing for the hit. Eventually daylight would weaken, the sun would recede from open sky and drop toward tree line, a soft orange glow of sunset would color the west, and the crows would fall silent, kick away from their branches and fly off toward the dimming light. A damp October chill would seep up from the ground, a last pass was thrown, and it fell time to retreat to your bike and pedal home for supper. And each fall, over the course of those ritual neighborhood bouts, the feel of those annual contests deepened, hardening toward something beyond mere sport.

Boy Scouts

"Crest has been shown to be an effective decay preventive dentifrice that can be of significant value when used in a conscientiously applied program of oral hygiene and regular professional care." There were some things kids committed to memory for no particular reason. The Crest ad on TV was one of them. The sentences were just words, sayings that didn't mean much. But everybody could parrot the toothpaste phrase verbatim.

"A scout is trustworthy, loyal, helpful, friendly, courteous, kind, obedient, cheerful, thrifty, brave, clean and reverent." The Boy Scout Law was like the Crest commercial. We memorized it long before we were old enough to become Boy Scouts. We could repeat it without thinking—the faster you recited the words, the more impressive the feat. So when I became old enough to join Scouts, I took the Scout Oath and recited the Law. But the words

90

were just habit, like brushing teeth at bedtime. I didn't think about the moral challenge of the Law because I didn't join Scouts to become cleansed. I joined because I wanted to go camping and have fun.

Thursday evening was Boy Scout night. Since 1926 Canfield had been home to Troop 25, Mahoning Valley Council of the Boy Scouts of America. So Thursday evening after supper I'd put on my pea soup green Scout uniform with red neckerchief, and Mom or Dad would drive me to town for the troop meeting.

About thirty of us scouts assembled in the basement of the Public Library at the south end of the green. In a long, narrow room with concrete floors and walls, the meeting always began with the same military drill. The Troop Leader and Assistant Troop Leader stood in front, facing the troop. The Troop Leaders were the oldest scouts— typically 10th or 11th graders. They were in charge of formation. Scouts in each patrol lined up together, at ease and standing shoulder to shoulder, with each Patrol Leader positioned two paces in front of his patrol. The troop thus formed a single line, from one end of the basement to the other, Patrol Leaders in front, for review by the Troop Leaders.

The Troop Leader would call the troop to attention, "AttenHUT!" and we'd snap straight and tall, head erect, shoulders back and arms to our sides. Then the Troop Leader would order the patrol reports, starting with the rightmost patrol in formation and working to the left. "Moose Patrol, rePORT!" came the order, and the Moose Patrol Leader would take three steps forward, execute a right face, march to the center of the room in front of the Troop Leader, pivot to him with a sharp left face, and salute. The Troop Leader would return the salute.

The Patrol leader would then report. "Eight present, six in uniform. Last patrol meeting we reviewed requirements for the wood carving merit badge, practiced knot tying and lashing, and planned next month's camp out at Lake Milton." The Troop Leader would acknowledge the report and dismiss the Patrol Leader with another salute. The patrol leader returned the salute, and retraced his march back to his position, ending his maneuver with a neat about face. Then the next patrol was ordered to report. The drill wasn't meant to be intimidating, but it could be a little unnerving, especially for younger scouts.

I started with the Raccoons and then the Moose Patrol, but when those groups grew too large I was assigned to the new Beaver Patrol. The early months of the Beavers were disorganized—weekly patrol meetings were haphazard and attendance was spotty. One Thursday evening I arrived at the troop meeting, having missed the patrol meeting earlier that week. I didn't want to miss the troop meeting on top of that. As scouts gathered in the basement before the meeting, talking with friends, I looked around for other guys in the Beavers. I didn't see anyone, but it was still ten minutes until opening drill. I didn't want to be the only Beaver there for formation. Someone else would come. I talked some more. At five minutes to formation—still no other Beavers, and I was getting uneasy.

"What if no one comes?" I thought. "I'll have to report the last patrol meeting, but I wasn't there." I didn't know what they did. I thought about it for moment. "No, I couldn't say I don't know. You're supposed to go to the patrol meetings—you're supposed to know what's going on," I thought. It would be embarrassing to admit I wasn't there. I struggled some more. "Maybe I could make something up, something simple … and then maybe we could do it at the <u>next</u> patrol meeting…." My mind was working hard. "If we did it next week, then it wouldn't exactly be a lie." I felt a little sweat in the curve of my back.

"Yeah, that might work," I thought. And I glanced anxiously about for a fellow Beaver. Then the Troop Leader's order rang out, "Line UP!" I looked one last time toward the door, but no more Beavers were coming. I was it. And turning in the back of my thoughts was that stubborn litany … "trustworthy, loyal, helpful, friendly…."

I lined up way down at the far left end. I wondered, "Should I line up back in the main row, or should I stand out in front where the Patrol Leader would stand?" I wasn't the Patrol Leader. I didn't know what the rules were--neither place seemed right. I wished I had stayed home. Since I was going to have to report, I decided I should stand in front. So I positioned myself two paces in front of my nonexistent patrol.

"AttenHUT!" the Troop Leader ordered. The troop stood silent as we came to attention. And "… courteous, kind, obedient, cheerful …" kept turning. I didn't know what I was going to say.

Starting at the far end of the line, the patrols marched through their maneuvers, salutes and reports, one after the other. We heard from the Moose, the Wolves and the Raccoons, all represented by at least five or six members at the meeting, and each Patrol Leader barked out an enviable patrol report about first aid drills, work on merit badges, or selling fire extinguishers door-to-door to raise money for new pup tents. At last they worked their way down to me. My time had come … "Beaver Patrol, rePORT!"

By then everyone knew I was the lone Beaver. So I heard some snickers as I marched forward, executed my turns, and positioned myself in front of the Troop Leader. I offered my best salute. The Troop Leader returned the salute and looked down at me.

"One present. One in uniform. Last patrol meeting I don't know what happened because I wasn't there." I felt stupid. A lie would have sounded much better and spared me the embarrassment. But the words just came out like that.

The Troop Leader tensed his face to keep his smile from turning into laughter. Then he looked at me and said, "Don't you think you should go to your patrol meetings?"

"Yes," I answered.

"Why don't you go back in line now." Then he added quietly, "You don't have to stand in front." And he saluted.

I returned his salute then marched back to the end of the troop. I did my about face and was relieved to merge back into the ranks.

They say scouting is supposed to build character. Maybe it does. Or maybe sometimes scouting just scares a little character out of you.

After that, I always made sure I knew what happened at patrol meetings.

James B. Jones was one of the oldest residents in Canfield—he was in his 90's. He and an elderly sister lived in one of those stately houses on the north end of the village green. Mr. Jones spoke slowly, was thin with narrow stoop shoulders and a full head of white hair. But even past 90 he was still agile--in good weather he was often seen walking about the village. He had been Mayor of Canfield around the turn of the century and carried forward the formality of those times, always dressed in suit and tie no matter the occasion.

Mr. Jones was a regular at Sunday services in the Methodist Church. They say he formed the first Boy Scout troop in the area in 1913, Canfield Troop 1. After Troop 1 disbanded following World War I, Mr. Jones helped form new Troop 25, and he remained active in scouting for decades thereafter. To earn the Forestry merit badge in Troop 25 in the 1960's, you had to pass your Forestry exam with Jimmy Jones.

For most of us scouts, dealing with someone as old as Jimmy Jones was a novelty. He was a kindly old guy, interested in scouting—a curiosity. We didn't see much more than that. Huey, the Moose Patrol Leader, told me that Mr. Jones' Forestry examinations were easy, and that when Mr. Jones completed the exam he would have you sit on his knee, call you "kidder" and talk a few minutes. Huey and I knew we were way too old for knee-sitting, and we laughed about the old man's peculiar ways. But "A scout is … friendly, courteous, kind…." And so like Huey before me, I figured I would just smile and be polite to Mr. Jones at my exam. It never crossed my mind that when you are almost one hundred years old, anyone less than fifteen probably seems like a child. It never occurred to us scouts that someday we, too, might become old. We were young--senility was a foreign land, and our endless futures didn't go there.

I recall standing on his front porch, waiting for Mr. Jones to come to the door when I arrived at his home for the merit badge exam. It was a pleasant summer day. He opened the screen door and emerged from a dark interior. It smelled a little musty inside. We exchanged greetings on his porch, and then I followed him out his front walk and across Broad Street onto the village green. He was dressed in suit and tie.

The exam consisted of walking from tree to tree on the north end of the green, attempting to identify each one. Ours was a slow walk. We methodically approached each tree, then paused beneath it to study the leaves and bark. We talked quietly about sugar maples, American elms, silver maples, hickories and white oaks. We proceeded from tree to tree, and I recognized most all of them until he said, "Now, let's go see something special."

We re-crossed Broad Street and walked to the knoll at the north end of the green, across from the Parkview House. There he pointed to a large tree next to an open, overgrown foundation, the site of an early Canfield home that no longer existed. The tree looked vaguely like a spruce, but had a strange needle I didn't recognize. I looked up and down the branches for cones, but didn't see anything familiar. Finally I admitted I didn't know what it was. "It's a baldcypress," Mr. Jones explained. It was a tree from the swamps deep in the South. It had been brought north and planted many years ago by an early Canfield resident. "This is the only tree of its kind in the entire village," he added.

We walked back to Mr. Jones' front porch and sat down. And sure enough, he had me sit on his knee and called me "kidder." It was embarrassing, but no one passing along Broad saw me, so I didn't mind much. We talked a few minutes, he told me I did just fine on my exam, and I thanked him. Then I left, and he went inside. A few weeks later at the awards ceremony for Troop 25, I received my Forestry merit badge.

As I walked the village green that day I had only one thing on my mind—identifying trees so I could get my badge. For me it was a matter-of-fact exercise in leaf shapes and bark texture. Being respectful of the old guy was an afterthought. But I realize now there was something more to our walk that day. For Mr. Jones our walk in the village went beyond inspecting leaves and meeting badge requirements.

For decades Jimmy Jones had looked out his front window upon those trees. He had moved among them when they were young, beginning to shoot upward. Over the years he watched them grow. He knew the pastels of their budding, the depth of their green limbs at summer, the flush of reds and yellows in the fall, and the strength of those branches against hard snows. He passed his life in the shade of those trees. And as he aged, as one by one his friends and neighbors dropped away, he hung on, growing more alone. And all the while, those trees continued to stand with him.

So as we walked about the maples and elms that day, we weren't just working on a scouting merit badge. For Mr. Jones, I believe our walk was a special visit. That day Jimmy Jones was introducing me to old friends.

It would be my first winter camping trip. Until then, we'd had only summer campouts, where cold was confined to that early morning chill before sunup. But one winter our Scoutmaster and Troop Leaders decided Troop 25 would confront real cold, and a February overnight was planned at Camp Stambaugh.

Stambaugh was a familiar place--a forested area several miles southeast of Canfield. Each July Troop 25 camped there for a week with surrounding troops from the Mahoning Valley. Stambaugh offered a number of campsites spread among the hills. Our February site was an open area with two cabins and several three-sided huts. Each cabin had a fireplace and bunk beds for about a dozen guys. The huts were for the more adventuresome. Each wooden hut had a floor, a sloping roof, two end walls and a side wall. But there was no fourth wall—on that fourth side, the east, the hut opened bare to the outdoors. Within the hut you were protected from snowfall and sheltered from prevailing westerly winds. You could build a fire on the ground, near the open side, for a little light at night. But the huts offered no protection from cold.

The campout was planned during several Thursday night troop meetings in the basement of the library. On the appointed Saturday, scouts would arrive at Stambaugh midafternoon and set up camp before sunset. We would prepare dinner over the fireplaces in the cabins, and then bed down for the evening. Each scout was to bring a sled from home, so the following morning after breakfast we could sled ride on some of the good hills in camp. We would leave late Sunday morning after sledding.

96

The weather on camping day was typical Ohio winter--a half foot of crusty snow lay on the ground, the temperature fixed around freezing, with the night forecast for clear skies, light winds and temperatures dropping into the 20's. The prospect of camping in the cold didn't bother me. I came prepared with two sleeping bags—one to stuff inside the other for double warmth. I wore several layers of clothes, and I was used to being outside in the winter--building snow forts, traipsing through frosty woods and ice skating on frozen ponds. So when we arrived at the site that afternoon and the Scoutmaster asked who would sleep where, I claimed a space in one of the huts, plopped down my pack and unrolled my sleeping bags on the wooden floor.

Scouts staying in my hut gathered kindling, chopped firewood and started a fire near the opening. Before dark set in, we stacked enough wood to keep the fire going through the night. Then Troop 25 gathered in one of the cabins for supper. It was comfortable in there--a big fire crackled away in the fireplace, the glow from the flames filled the room, and those soft bunk beds felt pretty inviting compared to the hard wood floor of my hut. But this was Boy Scouts at a winter camp out—it wasn't supposed to be comfortable. So when supper was through, with a touch of pride we hut sleepers left the warm light of the cabin and stepped outside into darkness.

That night I would begin to appreciate how there are two kinds of cold. I knew all about the first kind, the kind we encounter when the temperature drops and the creeks freeze and the snow falls. I was accustomed to that kind, where we bundle up in heavy coats and gloves and wool socks and step outside to confront the weather. We scurry against the cold from house to car, from car heater turned up to "High" into store, store back into the car and then home. The cold and chills make you shiver. But all the short bouts with cold have something in common—behind the shiver, back there somewhere rests the assurance that at day's end we will have shelter, the cold will stop and we will become again warm.

That night a new kind of cold would lay hold. This cold wouldn't emerge merely with the onset of low temperatures--a thermometer measuring it wouldn't register any different than the first kind of cold. This kind would come when a long winter night loomed and you realized there would be no relief, no shelter, no eventual warmth. You were vulnerable, exposed. And with that opening, the cold would begin to stir and then move to the attack--first your skin with frozen pin pricks, then deeper with icy needles, drawing warmth out of your surface, then out of your muscles. Eventually it would seek bone.

The guys in our hut finished talking, stoked up our fire and crawled into our sleeping bags. One by one, scouts began to fall asleep. But I couldn't sleep. Buried in my two sleeping bags with all my clothes on, I couldn't get warm. After a time, it began to hurt-- my legs were the worst. The cold worked deeper and my legs grew numb. I scrunched up in a ball and rubbed my calves. Then I hugged myself and rubbed my arms against my body, and rubbed and scrunched some more. But nothing worked—the cold kept coming. I tossed and scrunched and rubbed away into the night.

The fire beside the hut didn't help—when I got up and added wood and stood over the flame, the cold on my backside overpowered the meager warmth hitting my front. Bent against the fire, I looked across the clearing at the still cabin where we ate dinner. The windows were dark, and a wisp of smoke rose from the chimney. I thought about the warmth inside. But some mix of pride and scout's honor wouldn't let me give up. So I shivered and rubbed and suffered on into the darkness, wondering if this was what frostbite feels like.

In the morning others began to stir. My legs were numb from the knees down, and it felt odd to walk. But I didn't say anything. I held my legs over the fire, trying to regain feeling. A little heat from the flame began to sink in. I moved about, stiff-legged. But it wasn't until midmorning when we got our sleds and I tried running up and down the sledding hills, forcing blood to pump down to my toes, that the numbness began to retreat. My legs were still cold and my feet kind of numb a couple hours later when we broke camp, loaded up our gear, and headed back to town.

It took another day or so for my legs finally to thaw out and get back to normal.

Swimming was an important part of scouting. About once a month during summer, a swim at Neff's lake replaced Thursday troop meetings in the library basement. The Neff farm was on Lisbon Street, a half mile beyond the railroad tracks as you left the village. In a field behind the Neff house was a big farm pond for swimming.

It wasn't fancy. There was a small shanty of a couple rooms for changing. Nearby, a narrow wood plank diving board extended from the bank outward over the water about eight feet. A big vertical pipe on each side supported the plank about halfway out. The water at the end of the board was deep enough for diving if you didn't aim straight down. The plank had plenty of spring for good cannon balls and jack knives. A wooden raft about eight feet square was anchored in the middle of the lake. The raft floated upon 55 gallon steel drums. The lake water was pretty clear--underwater you could see out several feet--enough to know where you were going. They kept an old rowboat pulled up on shore, in case a swimmer had a problem. But it was never needed.

The first half of those Thursday evenings was free swim--just team up with a buddy and you could swim or dive as you pleased. The second half was competition among patrols. The Scoutmaster called it a wallakazoo—I think that was an Indian word for a contest. There were short freestyle sprints, long breaststroke races the length of the pond, backstroke races, underwater distance contests, and patrol relay races back and forth between the shore and the raft.

By the second year in scouts I had become a pretty good swimmer and helped score wallakazoo points for the Beavers. My favorite was the underwater distance swim. Each swimmer waited his turn to dive in near shore and swim underwater as far as he could toward a couple scouts positioned mid lake in the rowboat. Each swimmer before me popped up short of the boat. When it was my turn, I dove under and swam as hard and far as I could, trying to stay just a few feet below the surface. I was determined to win, and I took strong, fast strokes, one after another after another, until my lungs couldn't take it anymore, and then I took three more and

99

burst upward for air. As I broke through, I heard a couple Beavers shout—I had gone under the rowboat and came up a few yards beyond it. That was one of the few times we Beavers ever won anything.

We always finished the wallakazoo with a round of watermelon water polo. The game was played in shallow water, waist deep, along the shore. Everybody played, divided into two teams. The object was to grab the watermelon and splash and run and swim your way about thirty yards to the end zone. The other team tried to take the watermelon away and move it to the opposite end zone. If you were carrying the watermelon, the other team was allowed to grab you and hold you under until you let go of it. And then they would struggle to grab the bobbing melon and fight to carry it the opposite direction until your team swarmed in and tried to drown them to get the melon back.

After water polo, the troop quieted down and gathered on the bank. Draped in wet towels, troop leaders cut open the melon and passed out slices to everyone. The juice was a touch sticky, and the pink meat was crisp and sweet. In the aftermath of the contest, scouts relaxed, talked over the evening swim and tried to spit seeds farthest.

I liked the wallakazoo. But as for watermelon polo, I didn't think much of getting yanked under water and stomped on by a mob. There was no Boy Scout Law I could rely on which promised, "A scout is trustworthy, loyal, helpful ... and naturally buoyant." I liked the individual swimming a lot better, where I was more in control of when I came up for air.

7th Grade

The framework of school shifted in junior high. The old class lists signaling the first day of school disappeared, and the broad outline of the coming year vanished with them. Seventh graders were cast into new terrain with new ground rules, a moving maze that constantly prodded you down the hall toward next period.

With 7th grade we moved to the central section of the school building, on the first floor. The days of spending the entire school day in a single classroom with one teacher were done. Junior high mornings started with home room, a ten-minute administrative time for attendance and PA announcements. The bell then sounded, and you were off--three minutes to get to your first class. Home room wasn't homey, not like the old, familiar grade school desk where you lived during school hours. Instead, home room was more like home plate—the starting point where you entered the game and then took off toward first.

Movement ordered the day--three-minute bursts traveling the halls and corridors from room to subject to teacher to class. The intervals between movements--periods--numbered seven, each about fifty minutes, plus lunch. In English we had learned to place a period at the end of a sentence, signifying completion. But with seven successive periods, things were never complete. Even if you came to school with all homework done, there was always a loose end somewhere—an ongoing project in science or history, some approaching math test to worry about or book report requiring attention. There was no end to it.

Your new base of operations was your hall locker. That locker was the first place you went when you stepped off the bus in the morning and the final stop after the last bell at the end of the day. It was where you hung your coat, stacked your books and notebooks, stashed your sack lunch on the top shelf, and rummaged through the debris of old assignments frantically searching for that history report you completed yesterday that was now due next period. It was the place you cycled back to throughout the day, to drop off one set of books and pick up another before heading off again toward next class.

Corridors were lined with hundreds of those identical brown, steel lockers, each about five feet tall and a too narrow ten inches wide. Unless you were fortunate to be assigned one at the end of a bank of lockers, the only way to tell lockers apart was the tiny black number plate mounted on each locker door head high. On more than one 7th grade night the dreams came calling—the dream in which I searched hopelessly for locker 478 which somehow wasn't in line where it should have been or the dream where I stood before my locker, unable to recall the lock combination, my school world slipping into the abyss. Those nights, the whole construct of junior high rested upon a narrow, iffy foundation of getting inside that locker door.

Grade school teachers were women.   In 7th grade most of my teachers were men--Mr. Bernice for science, Taaffe in history, Mr. Wilhide for English, Mr. McLaughlin for gym, music with Rossi and Young for shop.   I didn't think having men teachers would make much difference, but I soon learned men teachers introduced a variety of new dimensions to school.

My grade school classmates and I began 7th grade at age twelve. By the end of the school year most 7th graders would turn thirteen—teenagers. Mr. Taaffe had a reputation for being tough— not out-to-get-you nasty, but blunt hard and to the point.   On the first day in his class, we filled out the usual forms, signed our names and passed the forms forward.   Mr. Taaffe looked them over, and when he came to mine he stood up, held my paper high overhead in front of the room and announced, "How am I supposed to know who Bob G. is? You're not in grade school, anymore," he scowled. "From now on use your last name when you sign your paper." Mike and Larry and Jane Ann and everybody else in the classroom knew who Bob G. was, but I got his point. He was serving notice that 7th grade would be different, and Mr. Taaffe wasn't going to take any guff from would-be teenagers. From where I sat, his announcement wasn't really necessary—I was already intimidated quite enough, thank you.

In grade school, the worst you had to fear from school was that school work would be hard. With Mr. Wilhide's 7th grade English class, school surpassed hard and entered the realm of demanding. Mr. Wilhide was slight build, modest, always in proper short sleeve white shirt and narrow tie, methodical and organized. He seemed to enjoy teaching and liked English.   But he believed in way too much homework and in assignments far more difficult than seemed fair. His tests necessitated days of study. Women teachers could assign a lot of work, too. But by the time my class entered junior high, most kids had come to understand student/teacher dynamics. As a result, each classroom usually included at least a few kids who could successfully whine and cajole and complain to women teachers for relief from burdensome assignments. But no matter how accomplished class whiners had become by 7th grade, there was no whining with Mr. Wilhide--only acceptance of his calm, firm expectations.

Early into that school year, I came to better appreciate Mr. Taaffe's first day "serving notice" tactic. Jack and I were standing next to his locker, talking. It was the end of the school day, the buses were outside loading up, and we were getting ready to leave. Our lockers were near the main exit to the bus circle, and all junior high and high school students used those main doors. Jack closed his locker and stepped backwards, accidentally bumping into a big high school guy cruising down the hallway. The guy had on a dark jacket with his hair slicked back. He stopped immediately and turned to size up Jack. Then suddenly the guy reached out, grabbed Jack by the collar and slammed him backward against the lockers in a steely crash. "What do you think you're doing, kid?" he snarled at Jack. Jack was speechless…. I just stood there with big eyes and my jaw hanging open. "You trying to mess with me, kid?" the guy said, leaning slowly forward and twisting Jack's collar.

Then instantly, out of nowhere Mr. Wilhide came flying down the hall, reached out and yanked the bully off Jack. The guy was caught completely off guard. "You come with me to the office!" Wilhide ordered the bully. He glanced over at Jack, "Are you OK?" Jack nodded. Mr. Wilhide turned and escorted the guy off by the scruff of his neck. Superman couldn't have done a better job.

Jack and I stood there a few seconds looking at each other, flustered. Then we realized we better get going or we'd miss our buses. So Jack finished with his locker, and we exited the big doors and walked down the front steps, grateful for Mr. Wilhide's hidden talents, thankful that Mr. Wilhide didn't take any guff, either.

The emphasis on academics in junior high was tempered with a few easy classes each week. Seventh graders were required to take music, gym and shop. Instead of shop, girls took home economics.

Music class with Mr. Rossi was conducted in the band room, on the backside of the high school behind the big auditorium. There we learned something of bands and orchestras, occasionally listened to classical music on the phonograph, and learned a little about reading notes and music. But since the majority of students didn't play an instrument, our primary activity was group singing of American folk classics. Our song book included old favorites like "Fifteen Miles on the Erie Canal," "My Darling Clementine," "I've Been Working on the Railroad" and "A Bicycle Built for Two." Girls sang the top part, boys sang the bottom.

After the first couple months of 7th grade, most kids were beginning to see how this junior high thing worked. Normalcy was returning--the more sassy guys in class were getting the hang of things and again starting to act up. A band room of forty would-be teenagers, feeling superior to the childish requirement of singing dumb folk songs, could have spelled trouble for Mr. Rossi—had it not been for a potent, lyrical punishment he was known to administer. If Rossi caught you misbehaving, clowning around when he wasn't looking, elbowing the person beside you or mocking a song, he'd immediately stop the group singing, turn to the offender and say, "All right, Mr. Dailey" (7th grade teachers often called students by last name, especially if you were doing something wrong), "I'd like you to sing verse three for everyone."

The Rossi solo was the kiss of death--that shut it down right there. The spectacle of a 7th grade music smart aleck blushing beet red, mumbling and stammering along, trying to singsong his way through "... but you'll look sweet, upon the seat, of a bicycle built for two" was not soon forgotten. The Rossi solo was more embarrassment than any macho 7th grader cared to face.

Mr. Rossi had found his own clever way of not taking any guff.

In 7th grade shop guys wore aprons. These aprons were nothing like the ruffled kitchen aprons girls wore in home economics. Our aprons were thick, manly covers of heavy blue cloth, the hue of Levis, a long strap around your neck with a big tie behind you, waist high. The firm material extended from chest to knee. It was designed to protect your school clothes from shop grit and metal filings, from splatters of paint, grease, acid and oil. If a photographer had lined us 7th graders up for a shop photo, he might

104

have thought us machinists behind those sturdy aprons, turning out steel dies for stamping sheet metal, or maybe skilled welders fabricating aircraft on an assembly line. But our 7th grade shop projects didn't quite measure up to labor of that stature. Rather, we employed our skills making dainty wooden napkin holders for mom.

I guess you had to start somewhere. Making a dinky napkin holder introduced basic woodworking skills--measuring, sawing, sanding, pounding finishing nails, and applying wood filler and varnish. But that was all simple, insulting stuff for those of us with years of experience constructing tree houses.

Seventh grade shop projects in metal were equally rinky-dink—cutting a flat piece of tin into a letter opener or using a hack saw and file to fashion a three-inch-long chunk of steel into the head of a small tack hammer. Such projects were little advanced beyond the commonplace plaster hand casts of grade school, or the arts and crafts projects of Cub Scout days. So if you somehow managed to slant your hack saw cut crooked or skew the alignment of the drill holes in your hammer head (which most of us did), shop class made you feel inept on top of rinky-dink.

If only we could have built something worthwhile, something cool—like a motorized go cart—shop might have permitted 7th grade guys at least a veneer of self-respect under those burly aprons.

Ketchup

In Boy Scouts, the Scoutmaster presented each new scout a good turn token, a gold-colored plastic coin about the size of a half dollar, stamped with the Boy Scout insignia. The token was a reminder of scouting's pledge to "Do a good deed every day." You started each morning with the token in your left hand pocket, so every time you reached into that pocket you'd be reminded of your obligation. Once you had done your good turn—like picking up trash from the floor of the school bus or helping your mom lug in the groceries— you'd shift the token to the pocket on your right side where you could then forget about it the rest of the day.

The Methodist Bible sitting on my bookshelf produced a similar effect as that token. Over the years it presided on the shelf, resting near a stack of Donald Duck comic books and Trains magazines, a silent reminder. And over time, the weight of Sunday sermons in the sanctuary, the example of respected adults in the congregation, and the power of deep organ notes on Easter morning pressed with the themes of that book—that there's a God out there looking over everything, he means business, and you better get on his good side.

Roast beef was my favorite. Mom sometimes bought a thick cut on her weekly visit to the grocery store. She prepared the roast for Sunday dinner, which we often ate in the dining room instead of the kitchen. If we had gone to church that morning, we usually still had on church clothes. Always Mom served the roast in big pieces of well done meat that came apart easy with your fork. The peas or carrots, mashed potatoes and gravy, green beans or fresh tomatoes were sidelights—the centerpiece of the meal was that big chunk of roast beef.

Roast beef tasted best plain—maybe with a little salt and pepper, but nothing else to change the taste. Its flavor was rich and dark, with a gush of juiciness when you bit down into the warm muscle. The meat wouldn't disappoint you—on Sunday you could count on that strong, full taste. But then, one Sunday dinner, I decided to try a little ketchup on a piece of roast beef. The transformation was remarkable. Just a little ketchup changed everything.

The ketchup taste took over the beef. It jumped out and covered the dark meat taste with a tang, a sharpness. Some beefy taste was still there, but it got pushed into the background, more of an aftertaste once the ketchup had its way. It was no longer the pure roast beef which I had enjoyed for years—it was a different, new taste, and I had to admit it was good. From that point forward, Sunday dinners required a choice—plain roast beef or beef with ketchup?

Religion was like ketchup on roast beef. Like most kids, I just took each new day as it was served up—simple and plain, like roast beef. I didn't know any better, and each day offered much to enjoy. But when you added in the flavor of religion, even only a little, the new, tangy taste took over. And that sensation, of being right with God, pushed aside the full, everyday, meaty plainness, till little remained of the old familiar main course.

Plain roast beef or beef with ketchup? You had to decide. I shifted over to ketchup.

School Skate

Before there were high school proms, there were school dances. Before there were school dances, there were junior high sock hops. And before junior high sock hops, there were Saturday skates in the old gym. Dances and sock hops were for girls, not guys—guys could care less about dancing. But a skate wasn't quite the same as a dance. I felt roller skating didn't qualify as a true sport, but I appreciated that it took coordination and skill to skate well. So a Saturday roller skate at school seemed like it might actually be OK.

I could ice skate well enough, thanks to lots of winter practice on our pond at home. Ice skating techniques differed from roller skating, but enough carried over that I could get by on wheels. Even more importantly, at Saturday skates you could skate by yourself--you didn't have to feel like one those awkward guys at dances who never ventured out from the guy corner, afraid to ask someone to dance because she might say "No." Mom, Carol and Nancy knew about the skates. They encouraged me to go and eventually convinced me. So one Saturday I gave the school skate a try.

I liked the old gym, the same place that served as school cafeteria during the week and the location of our big Christmas tree sing-alongs back in grade school. The hardwood floor was nicked and beat down, the finish long since worn away, but the room was plenty big for fifty or sixty kids to skate round and around in a circle. Stopping quickly was hard for me, since you couldn't dig in the wheels like you could blades on ice. But I was able to control generally where I was going. Records blared out over the PA from a boxy speaker mounted near the ceiling above one of the basketball backboards.

The skate was going fine until a voice came on the PA system and announced "Girl's Choice." I hadn't counted on that. I came to a stop. Quick out of the blue Paulina skated up to me and stopped. I had noticed her skating earlier in the afternoon and thought her skating was really good. But I hadn't paid any more attention to her. Paulina didn't say anything standing there in front of me, but motioned for me to take her hands and join her. Without thinking, I did, and she pulled me into the circle. The music started, and like that we had our arms crossed somehow in front of us and were skating around the floor with others.

I knew Paulina from school—she was in 7th grade, too--but I didn't pay any attention to her there, either. I never bothered with her. She had always been one of those names you looked past on the class lists at the beginning of the school year. In 7th grade she took different subjects and classes, and I had nothing to say to her. I was surprised she wanted to skate with me.

Around the gym we went. My skating was awkward, while hers was strong and graceful. She pulled me along to the music, weaving and guiding us about, around the floor with skill and style. Neither of us said anything.

When the record was done, we stopped and both let go. I should have said something then, like "Thanks for the skate," or "Gee, you're a good skater." But I didn't. I wasn't trying to be mean—but I was at fault for not trying to be even a little polite or considerate. I should have said at least a little something.

But no words were exchanged. So she turned aside and skated off.

The following week in school, neither of us said anything to the other. I guess we were too bashful or hurt or embarrassed. So we ignored each other.

Years later Paulina and I graduated in the same class. But after that Saturday skate, I don't believe either of us said a word to the other the rest of the way through school.

Pony League

Little League players advanced to Pony League. Not everybody went on—by twelve or thirteen the guys who weren't too serious about baseball dropped away. So there were fewer teams than in Little League, and the focus on baseball skills increased. It wasn't the majors. But overall fielding improved, errors were much reduced, pitchers began to develop curve balls and knuckle balls along with the standard fare fast ball, and batters needed a keener eye and quicker swing. The schedule included a few games against teams in neighboring towns: we played a couple games in North Lima behind their high school, and once traveled to Lowellville, a ball field down along the Mahoning River beside the busy tracks of the B&O.

I played a couple years of Pony ball on the Canfield Merchants team. Our field was near the old Little League field, along the same dirt road off Lisbon Street, just past Delf's. Compared to the Little League outfield, the Pony home run fence was a mile away—no matter how lucky I got, I knew I was never going to hit a ball that far, so I didn't even try. A solid hit and getting on base was my batting goal. I continued to play right field, but I also spent some time in center and occasionally the coach played me at second. I could handle pop ups, fly balls, line drives and most grounders pretty well. While fast grounders at second could be a problem, I didn't make too many more errors than others on the team.

At some stage back in Little League the fun of playing baseball began to fade--replaced by an emphasis on competition. With Pony League, that emphasis reached its logical conclusion—the need to win. In Pony it wasn't enough to field a grounder well and make a good throw to first. No, you had to get the runner out--your throw had to beat him. You needed to get a hit, not because you wanted to get a hit, but because your team needed to score runs. The game became the exercise, the means to the end; the main thing was winning.

With this focus on competition, someone unfamiliar with Pony League might imagine that at the first practice each player would be issued a heavy three-ring binder entitled "Winning." The binder would be brimming full with stories and analysis of what winning is all about, why victory is so important. Chapter One would lay the groundwork, setting forth the curious human fascination with two opposing forces locked in struggle. Chapter Two would analyze how "winning" was merely a comfortable term, instead distilling the word to its essence--successfully inflicting your will on another, against his. Three would examine how the term "sports" colors that conflict acceptable--so much so the contest becomes a celebrated social activity. And Chapter Four would explore why competition intensifies as we evolve from known teams of our Little League youth, where opponents are friends, to unknown teams comprised of nameless adversaries from other towns.

Of course there were no three-ring binders. They weren't needed. From Pony coaches and parents we still heard the old encouragements "Just do your best" and "It's not whether you win or lose, it's how you play the game." But by Pony League, kids knew better. We could see how the world worked. We knew what we felt when we had to return to the field after losing, trying to act like a good sport, lining up and congratulating the winners. Nobody wanted to be a loser. Winning beat the heck out of losing.

That first year of Pony ball was best. Bobby and Richy from Meadowview days were on the team, along with Mike, Jeff and a half dozen other guys from my grade. The rest of our team was a bunch of good players from the grade ahead of us. Ted was all muscles and a dependable catcher—his dad, Mr. Dyckman, coached. Gary was our ace pitcher. And we had some strong guys who could hit the ball hard. With Gary and Ted at the heart of our solid lineup, the Canfield Merchants pounded through the schedule that season, knocking down most of the opposition. But we weren't the only good team in the league—Wilson Pontiac out of North Lima was good, too. By the end of the season, with one game remaining, we were tied with Wilson for the best record. Our last game would be against Wilson for the league championship.

Game day was sunny and warm, with a dry field. We were at home, working out of the dugout next to third. Gary walked to the mound, and I trotted into the outfield as Canfield players took up position. Everyone knew what was at stake, and tensions were high. A small crowd of parents and spectators was on hand, and they were treated to a good game.

It was a pitcher's duel. Wilson had a few guys who could really slam the ball, but Gary contained them. And Wilson's ace pitcher threw hard and fast, so it was tough going at the plate for both teams. Walks were few, and strikeouts many. By the late innings, each team had managed to score only a couple runs on scattered hits.

The score was tied when Canfield came to the dugout for our at bats. It was the bottom of the next to last inning. If we could get a run, and then Gary could hold them off for one more inning, we would win. I checked the lineup on the coach's clipboard hanging from the dugout wall and confirmed I'd be up fourth. If somebody could get on base before me, I'd have an at bat. I was nervous thinking about it, and knew I'd be a lot more nervous if I actually got to the plate.

Wilson's pitcher made quick work of our leadoff man—struck him out without much trouble. The batter returned to the dugout in silence. One down. Richy was up next. He batted left, was a little taller than me, probably twenty pounds heavier, and thanks to all our practicing back on Meadowview, he was a decent hitter. "Come on, Rich, you can hit him, get on," we all encouraged as he left the on deck circle and entered the batter's box. I'm sure his heart was pounding just like mine.

Richy had a slow, methodical manner when he stepped up to the plate. He took his time and motioned the bat around slowly a couple times before he settled in for the first pitch. "Ball!" the umpire shouted. Then I remembered Big Tom would be up after Richy, which meant I would need to be ready to enter the circle. I started poking around the dugout to get a helmet and find my 31 inch bat. A moment later I was sorting through the bats when I heard a whack and the team let out a yell. I looked up to see a line drive dropping into left center—a hit!--and Richy was running to first. The outfielders chased after the ball, and Richy headed to second. He pulled up there with the throw from the outfield. We had a runner on, which meant I'd probably have an at bat. I took a deep breath trying to stay calm.

Big Tom took his 34 inch bat, left the on deck circle and walked to the plate. I grabbed my bat and went to the circle. Tom was a year older than Richy and me. He wasn't our best hitter, but he was several inches taller than I was and forty pounds heavier. He had been through a few more baseball wars and could drive the ball deep. Along with fans and players, the coach shouted encouragement, "Let's go! Come on Tom, you can do it! Be a hitter!" And the coach clapped his hands.

The first pitch came fast—Strike One! Tom stepped out of the batter's box. You could see he was feeling the pressure, but we knew he was good enough to drive in that run. With him at the plate, there was hope.

I thought about my chances at the plate. I sometimes got a hit, but it didn't happen a lot. Wilson's pitcher was really fast, and I hadn't done anything against him with my other at bats. At that moment if you held a Magic 8 Ball and asked "Will Gentzel get a hit?" then shook it and turned it over, the 8 Ball surely would have replied "My sources say no."

"Ball!" came the umpire's call.

"Good eye! Make him work!" we all shouted to Tom. The count was even at one and one.

Then it dawned on me ... "The coach won't let me bat. He knows I'll probably make an out. Sure—there're other guys on the bench who can hit—they'd have a better chance than I would. He'll put somebody else in to pinch hit for me." Tom swung hard—Strike Two! "Yeah, he'll yank me--that's what Mr. Dyckman will do," I reasoned. "He'll pull me and have someone else hit."

Tom waited for the next pitch. Richy took a cautious lead from second. The pitcher checked the runner, stared down Tom and then began his windup. The ball came burning at the plate, and Bob swung fast. "Strike Three! You're Out!" the ump shouted. Two outs....

I turned to the dugout, expecting to see Coach Dyckman motioning me back. But he didn't--it didn't happen. "OK, let's go, Bobby!" the coach clapped. "Let's get a hit, be a hitter now!" It didn't make sense. And the team urged me on. No pinch hitter--I was wrong. It would be up to me.

As Tom walked back to the dugout and passed, he urged quietly, "Come on, Bobby." I walked toward the plate. If he couldn't get a hit, I didn't know how I could.

It's comforting to a nervous ballplayer that no matter how big the game, how intense the pressure, the roles for every player are clearly scripted. You don't have to guess—you always know exactly what to do. Every act revolves around that ball. The pitcher knows where to throw it. The batter knows where to stand, when to swing, where to hit it. The outfielders know to move to the ball, how to field it and where to throw it. The infielders know the base to protect and the runner to attack. And the runners know the prescribed path to follow. All that orchestration is preset—you can count on it every time, a complex chess game of sorts, where each pitch sets all the pieces into motion at once. It's only the success of the execution of each move, each action, that's in doubt.

So as I entered the batter's box, I didn't worry about what I was supposed to do—that was clearly established. But fear of my impending execution loomed large.

I looked out over the field. Wilson's infield was playing back a little, and their shortstop was in his normal position—he wasn't trying to hold Richy close to second. Wilson needed just one more out, so they were betting on keeping the ball in the infield and throwing me out at first. Although Wilson's pitcher was fast, I knew if I had any chance of meeting the ball, it was probably going to go toward left, since I usually swung early. I noticed the left fielder was playing way back—I couldn't hit a ball all the way to where he stood if my life depended on it. But I sure wasn't going to tell him to move in. I checked the sign from our third base coach—Swing away. A little dust blew across the infield.

The first pitch came—high and fast, and I swung and missed. Strike One! As soon as the pitcher released the ball I saw it was way too high, but I just couldn't hold back when it flew at me. I moved away to catch my breath, and the Merchants cheered me on. I stepped back in the box and went through my ritual batting motion a few times, waiting on the pitcher to settle in. He checked on Richy then began his warm up. I readied to swing, and a bullet came firing home chest high. I swung fast and hit it in the air toward left. I dropped the bat and took off, then glimpsed left to see what was happening. It was a weak liner over the shortstop, the left fielder was coming in hard, Richy was nearing third, and our dugout was screaming "RUN! RUN!" The ball was hanging in the air, and the left fielder stretched his glove low and was almost to it. "He's gonna catch it!" I thought. But the ball dropped that last foot, hit the grass and bounced up into his glove. Richy was clearing third and the team was jumping and screaming him home. "GO! GO! Come ON!!! GO!!" I rounded first and slowed to see where the fielder was throwing. He came up with the ball and heaved it home.

Richy was nearing the plate, and I took off to second. The ball was almost to the catcher when Richy slid past him and tagged home. "SAFE!!" the ump signaled.

From my perch on second, I watched the eruption of clapping and jumping and yelling in the dugout and stands as Richy stood up and the team burst out and mobbed him. I was jumping up and down, too, waving arms overhead in celebration of my big hit. Wilson's second baseman was standing right beside me. I thought maybe I was showing off a little bit with the arms, so I lowered my arms and just continued clapping and shouting. It felt pretty good.

Things settled down and the game resumed. I didn't get past second. Our next batter struck out and the inning was over. Despite our celebration, the game wasn't won quite yet, so Canfield took the field a final time. And Gary came through--he held them scoreless for the win and the championship. I didn't think about what Wilson's last batter must have felt when he was thrown out at first to end the game—I was too busy jumping up and down cheering.

It's a curious thing. The more improbable the outcome, the more we celebrate the event. If you hold a baseball in your hand and release it, the ball falls to earth. It happens every time. And we know gravity is awfully important—without it, we wouldn't be here. Yet we never celebrate gravity's simple thud when a dropped ball hits against the ground. But take that ball and construct around it a set of complex rules and parameters, mix a tiny part of hope into the equation, and stir in a high probability of failure, and the thud of that ball on the earth can spark quite a celebration.

Coach Dyckman was happy with our win. I imagine baseball strategy dominated his thinking during the game—setting up the batting order, positioning players in the field, deciding when to pinch hit, and signaling when to bunt or sacrifice to advance a runner. But once play began, for him the contest might have seemed more like a session of pinball than baseball. He'd carefully pull back on the spring-loaded launcher, insert a batter at the plate, then release the spring, launching his player to go rolling and ricocheting into the maze.   Mindful of the odds, uncertain of the outcome, hopeful in the trajectory …

Like his players, Coach Dyckman wanted to win, and he calculated his actions accordingly.   But unlike his kids, he knew sometimes it could be more important to let hope guide your hand.

Cowboys and Indians

It began as a joyful romp, like spring puppies frolicking in the grass, rolling and yipping with playful leaps.

You'd run and dive headlong into the tall weeds, your cap gun drawn and cocked as you crouched low against the ground.   You knew they were coming—that bunch of lowdown varmints--and you were ready for them.   Hidden, the element of surprise was on your side.   And you breathed quietly, waiting….   And when the bad guys came running around the corner of the house, you let them have it with everything you had, blasting away!   And the air was pierced with hot lead and echoing cries of "I got you! You're dead! No you didn't!! I got you first! Uh huh, yes I did."   Then, as the volleys of shot slowed and the mortal debates died away, fighters would break rank and the two sides scattered—one to the backyard and the other band retreating up the street to the neighbor's.   There, fighters would rest, regroup, reload and plan the next attack.

Nothing was more fun than playing Cowboys and Indians. Everything about it--the threat of danger around the next bend, the chase, lying in wait and the surprise attack—was charged with energy, with spark that made the game more than simple pretend— made it real.

Maybe we owed it to the Lone Ranger, the Cisco Kid and that stampede of TV cowboys in the 50's.   I soon wore out my yellow Davy Crockett T-shirt, the one with Fess Parker standing before the Alamo, Old Betsy held defiantly across his chest.   I watched all the shows … "Last of the Mohicans," "Maverick," "Wagon Train," "Cheyenne" and "Sugarfoot."   And it seemed perfectly normal that "The Wonderful World of Disney" would air episodes of Texas John Slaughter on Sunday evening for family viewing.   His ballad promised "Texas John Slaughter, made them do what they oughter, and if they didn't they died"—nothing to raise an eyebrow there.   In those days Wild Bill Hickok and Marshall Dillon seemed to mount up

115

and ride on more than just horseflesh--they galloped along on some deeper chord that stirred their audiences. Whatever it was, each episode pulled me along.

By the age of seven or eight, squirt guns replaced cap guns as the weapon of choice. True, with squirt guns you sacrificed those exploding cap bangs in the heat of battle. But that little trigger mechanism which advanced the roll of caps when you fired was unreliable. It often failed to push the next cap into place, or it jammed up the red paper roll when you most needed to shoot. Squirt guns were more dependable, and you could actually hit someone when you shot. Squirt guns put an end to all those battleground debates over who shot whom first. The one drawback to squirt guns, of course, was they didn't have the same range as cap guns. With a maximum squirt of 15 or 20 feet, you couldn't shoot someone clear across the yard. So squirt guns led to more close in fighting, more point blank soggy encounters.

By about age eight, Christmas lists began including a Marx battle play set from the Sears catalogue. First the Alamo, then a year or two later Wagon Train, then Fort Apache—the large flat boxes contained dozens of two-inch plastic figures and battle accessories. There were fighting frontiersmen, Indians, Mexican soldiers and Confederates, forts and barricades, teepees and campfires, galloping horses, covered wagons and cannon. I commanded my forces in long basement battles: a pitched attack on a wagon train by Mexicans and renegade Indians, a daring escape by the settlers to the safety of the fort, then a long and withering siege, and finally the Union cavalry riding to the rescue.

Playing soldiers in the basement was different from the running squirt battles of earlier years. Moving each piece across the cement floor was a carefully crafted production, far more calculated than plotting sneak attacks against the band of neighborhood desperados up the street. But the energy of the fight and the sweep of the battle remained compelling. The ebb and flow of the contests could last for hours. I staged attacks and counterattacks, cavalry flanking movements and full frontal assaults. And always it ended with victors and routed foes.

Safely above the battle lines, pushing horses and regiments and cannon right and left, I might have felt like a battleground god, except for one thing. The play sets never contained dead people. The soldiers were always shooting or marching, the Indians always running and waving their tomahawks and spears, the settlers forever locked into position walking calmly beside the wagon or driving oxen. So even if you knocked figures over to try to kill them, on the ground they were still running or shooting or walking—just doing it now at an awkward, different angle. You couldn't kill those plastic figures. There was no blood. Nobody ever died.

In grade school we used the town fire siren for civil defense drills. The siren was a big round cylinder, like a barrel, mounted on the roof of the fire station, a block from school. Now and then the siren would commence and wail out across the village, calling volunteer firefighters. It blasted a deep tone, rising then falling then rising again, up and down and up and down until the firemen arrived. Then the siren switch was turned off and the deep wail began to weaken. In a few moments, the smaller sirens on the fire trucks rose up and took over, and then the engines pulled out of the house, turned onto Lisbon Street, and rushed away. As the engines sped off, it took a long minute for the fading pitch of the big siren to recede lower and lower, softening into the background, and finally restoring quiet.

For civil defense drills, the siren was activated at a set time, and then it just kept wailing. Teachers explained each drill to us in advance, so we knew when it was going to happen and what to do. A drill was a welcome break from normal classroom routine. I didn't understand why grade school conducted practices as much as they did. The drill wasn't difficult—we kids all knew how to crawl under our desks. There was no urgency or shouting or commotion. The procedure was matter-of-fact, a simple 1-2-3 process: hear the siren, slide out of your seat, and crawl under your desk.

But sometimes during the drills, crouched down under the desk, it seemed the siren was wailing too long—much longer than when it summoned firemen. It kept blaring out across the village, against the quiet, piercing the stillness, but nothing was happening. We kids just kept crouching there motionless, listening, waiting ... And sometimes, just for an instant, something in the air didn't feel right, something seemed off ... eerie. Fortunately the feeling was fleeting—it didn't last. Always, eventually, the rising and falling stopped, the wail began to subside, weaken, and gradually it fell away to rest. The drill was over, everything felt OK again, and we climbed back into our seats.

When I was about eleven or twelve, one day I opened the small bookcase at home and pulled down Life Magazine's Picture History of World War II. I knew some things about the war. On Palmyra Road Carol, Nancy and I had sometimes watched formations of stubby World War II cargo planes lumbering west above the woods. They always flew in groups of three, six or nine. Mom and Dad called them "flying boxcars." Mom's brothers had fought in France, and Dad had been in the Coast Guard. I kept a picture of his ship, the SS Action, in my bedroom on the bookcase. He sailed back and forth between New York and Cuba, escorting convoys. I think once or twice they ran into German submarines. Next to the ship photo was a model B-17 which I built from a plastic kit.

I paged through the history book, the pictures of tanks, planes and soldiers, and looked at maps showing battle lines across North Africa and Europe, and photos of ships to the horizon on D-Day. I was fascinated with the scenes. Then I came to a photo of a pile of bodies lying in a street. It was grotesque and unreal, nothing I could ever imagine. I looked at a few more pages, then closed the book and put it back in the bookcase. I tried not to think about it. I told myself the war was a long time ago and the picture was somewhere far away. It couldn't happen here. I forced the image out of my mind.

One Monday evening a year or two later, I got up from my bedroom desk for a homework break and walked into the living room. Mom and Dad were sitting on the couch watching television. I heard President Kennedy talking, and I noticed the look on my parents' faces--never before had I seen expressions like that. The President was talking about Cuba and missiles, and Mom and Dad were intent on the message. I listened for a few minutes until his address was done. And the reality of his words began to sink in for me, as it had for my parents. There was no ignoring it, no pretending.

Mom and Dad understood Kennedy's words in ways I never could. I'm sure Mom sensed the difference between my Cub Scout ashtray next to her on the end table and youth groups in Germany years before. Dad understood how lives change when fighting starts. They knew what it meant, what happens when Cowboys and Indians grows up. In that look in their faces, those <u>Life Magazine</u> war pictures from decades before and a world removed drew uncomfortably close.

I couldn't hear it, but in that moment I sensed somewhere a siren was wailing, on and on and on. And the solid ground underneath shuddered way down deep.

8th Grade

Despite all the changes to school routine with the onset of junior high, a few things remained constant. In 8th grade, as in 1st grade, the highlight of the school day was recess. In junior high, the familiar grade school aspects of recess were modified. The name was altered—now it was disguised as gym or Physical Education. You changed into play clothes in the locker room before, and you showered and changed back to school clothes afterward. Girls and guys had separate gym classes, and gym teachers encouraged you to use deodorant after you showered. Phys Ed activities were more organized and fixed around rules than monkey bar climbing or playground games of tag in grade school. But at its essence, gym was still recess.

Phys Ed class started with a few calisthenics—jumping jacks, pushups and toe touches. Then we spent the rest of the period in a planned activity like tumbling, gymnastics on parallel bars, basketball, volleyball or wrestling. Guys enjoyed playing all the sports, but for sheer fun, you couldn't beat gym dodge ball.

In grade school, dodge ball was tame. The teacher supervised. Classmates formed a circle with a group of kids inside, and you took turns rolling a big ball at the kids in the middle, trying to hit them so they'd have to leave the circle. The last person left in the middle was the winner. The goal of gym dodge ball was the same—be the last man standing. But with that, similarities between the versions ended.

Gym dodge ball was a free-for-all swirling around a few basic rules. The class was divided into two teams, one on each end of the gym. Throughout the game, you had to stay on your end of the gym, behind the basketball center court line. Each team was given three volleyballs, and play commenced. The object was to throw and hit a guy on the other team, knocking him out of the game. But if he caught your ball in the air, you were out. With thirty guys hurling a half dozen balls back and forth, opposing throwers running to center line and winging balls in point blank duels, others hanging back dodging throws, balls slamming into walls, and guys jumping to snag whizzing fastballs overhead, you had to move fast.

As the game narrowed to a handful of players, action shifted from a rapid-fire test of reflex to a more deliberate contest. Two or three guys on the same team could gang up on a lone opponent, trying to nail him in a massive barrage. If the game was down to a single player on each side and you controlled all the balls, you could move center court and fire them in quick succession at the surviving opponent. But you better throw hard and low so that misses bounced off the wall right back to you, or the enemy would gather those balls and come running mid court to counter attack.

A fast volleyball in the face really stung. But that didn't matter. Dodge ball was the most fun you were allowed in school.

By junior high, those neighborhood football scrimmages after school had evolved into more. The guys now ran faster and hit harder. We had learned to fend off blockers, to catch over-the-shoulder passes and to bring down even the biggest players by tackling them low and wrapping up their knees. You could still get banged up. But everyone was stronger, could take more punishment and had learned how to dish out hits, as well. Richy, Bobby, Danny and I were beginning to think we might try out for freshman football—the first chance in those days to play organized football. I wasn't completely sure about trying out, but any uncertainty I had about playing freshman ball was laid to rest one day in 8th grade gym.

On fall days, we sometimes went out back to the varsity football field for gym. After calisthenics we divided into two teams to play flag football, a watered-down version of real football. Here the main goal was for students to avoid injury so everyone could report to his next class. We wore no helmets or protective equipment--

120

just tennis shoes, our gym outfits and a plastic belt with a small flag snapped to the belt at each hip. Instead of tackling a runner, you yanked off his flag. With thirty guys in gym class, a big crowd clumped around the ball every play.

I enjoyed flag football and wanted to be in the middle of things. On one particular day my team was on defense, and I was playing back, protecting against the pass. With the snap, the opposing quarterback dropped back and launched a long pass toward a couple ends going deep. The ball arched through the air and began angling downward. I raced to the middle of the pack of players massed to go up for it. As I jumped and stretched toward the spinning ball, a feeling surged over me. Some floodgate seemed to open, and I wanted to grab that ball more than anything else in the world! In that second, that's all there was. There was no up or down, no this way or that, no tomorrow or yesterday—nothing except me and that ball. The urge to catch it was everything. And I tore the football out of the air amid a sky of flailing arms and elbows, hit the ground and took off as fast as I could.

The feeling of that moment, being consumed by that ball twisting through the air, stuck with me. Maybe that's how a dog feels when you throw a stick and he leaps after it with abandon. Or maybe it's the same urge that compels a salmon headlong into the rapids.

I don't know. But with that instant, football had me.

Lifesaving

One summer I earned the Boy Scout merit badge for swimming, along with the Mile Swim at Camp Stambaugh. The camp lake wasn't a mile wide, but two end points had been measured out, and with enough patience you could cover a mile swimming back and forth. After the Mile Swim, the next step was to earn the Lifesaving merit badge. So the following year at summer camp I signed up for Lifesaving.

Lifesaving class was the first activity after breakfast. Class started when the sun had barely risen above the trees surrounding the lake, so the water was cold and the air a little colder. Unlike Neff's pond, water in Lake Stambaugh was stirred and muddy—a soupy light brown. You couldn't see through the goop more than a foot.

Half a dozen scouts from different troops had signed up, and Monday morning we assembled at the dock for our first class. Most of the guys were a little bigger than me. Our instructor was an older scout—he had earned the Lifesaving badge a couple years earlier. The first day we covered artificial respiration and some basic lifesaving techniques--how to approach a struggling swimmer, how to avoid being pulled under and the best way to move a calm person to shore. We took turns jumping in and performing the maneuvers, and after each turn you climbed back onto the dock to shiver until it was your next turn. The cold made it unpleasant, and the swimming was a challenge, but I kept up OK.

Tuesday morning was cold again, and the class resumed where we had left off on Monday. We paired up for more swimming drills, with one guy the rescuer and the other scout playing victim. After about an hour of diving and swimming against some pretend thrashing by victims, the instructor gathered us on the end of the dock for the last drill of the morning. He pointed to a big cement block resting beside us on the dock boards. It was caked in mud and a little moss, and looked heavy--maybe 20 to 25 pounds, the kind of cement block used to construct new foundations. One end of a muddy rope two feet long was tied to it.

"All right," the instructor said. "This block is a drowning swimmer. I want each of you to dive in after it and bring it up off the bottom and put it back here on the dock." And he lifted the block and heaved it out into the water. It landed with a dirty splash about eight feet away. A swirl of bubbles marked the spot for a moment, and then it sank and disappeared. The water where it went down was about seven feet deep. "This is a requirement," he announced. "You need to do this to earn the merit badge. OK, who wants to be first?"

I wasn't eager, so I waited. "I'll go," one of the other scouts said. We watched as he took a couple deep breaths and dove in. Twenty seconds later he popped back up, without the block. "I can't find it," he said, treading water off the corner of the dock.

"Try again," the instructor said.

So the scout took a couple more deep breaths and went back down. After another twenty seconds he surfaced again, without the block. "Can't find it."

"All right," the instructor answered. "Come on out and let someone else try. You can try again, later." The first scout swam back to the dock and climbed up the short ladder. "OK, who's next?" the instructor asked.

A second scout volunteered and dove in. But when he popped up the result was the same—he couldn't find the block. He caught his breath and then dove down to try again. After fifteen or twenty seconds he came back up, still empty-handed. He climbed the ladder back onto the dock.

"You guys are going to have to keep trying till you do this," the instructor reminded us. He seemed to enjoy telling us. "OK. Who's going next?"

A third scout dove in. Fifteen seconds later we saw some churning in the water from underneath where he dove, it continued for a bit, then he broke the surface with a splash. "I found it," he panted, "but couldn't get it up." He had raised it part way, but had to release it to come up for air. After a minute he caught his breath and dove back after it. When he surfaced he shook his head, "I couldn't find it this time."

Another guy tried, and the result was the same—no cement block. I didn't think it should be that hard to find, but apparently feeling around down there in the bottom mud was tougher than I imagined. Finally I said, "I'll go."

I dove in--almost straight down--to where I thought it should be. My eyes were open but I couldn't see a thing. I felt the bottom come to me and began moving my arms around, spreading them back and forth over the muck. I moved this way and that, hoping to hit into it. After fifteen seconds or so of nothing but muddy bottom, my lungs were starting to strain--I would have to surface soon. I was about to quit and head up when the back of my arm hit something. I reached for it and felt the edge of the block and the knotted rope. My air was short and I needed to go up, but I had to try. I grabbed the block with one arm, moved my feet under me into the muck and pushed up. I kicked and pulled upward at the water with my free arm, but the block weighed me down—it resisted hard. I struggled against the cement and my lungs were urging "Breathe!" I kicked and swam as hard as I could, and I got closer to the surface. I almost let go, but I kept thrashing and fighting up. Finally my arm broke the surface. I strained my mouth up as far as I could to find air, and gasped and spit air and water. I gulped air, but the weight of the block pulled my mouth back under. I bent knees way up to tread water and keep my mouth up, gasping and spitting and trying to pull myself toward the dock. I splashed and thrashed my way nearer the dock, as they all stood there calmly watching me battle. At last I managed a final stroke and reached out to grab the ladder. I pulled myself over to it, raising my head now safely out of the water. I was breathing hard as I climbed the couple rungs of the ladder, lugging the block against my stomach, upward out of the water. Then I wrestled the cement over the edge of the boards and slid it onto the dock. I climbed the rest of the ladder and stood again with the group.

"See that," the instructor said to the others. "All the bigger he is and he did it." I just stood there dripping and panting.

I didn't return to Lifesaving class on Wednesday. I chickened out. True, where some had failed, I had succeeded in rescuing the cement block. And maybe I could have made it through the next three days and earned the merit badge. But that struggle scared me off.

From early on, life seems all about things that could be. You can be a pirate, or shoot like the Lone Ranger, or fly like Peter Pan. Grownups ask each of us, "What do you want to be when you grow up?" And the doorways ahead seem open wide. I was probably about four when I came up with the idea there might be a way to make my muscles really, really hard, to tighten them so much and make myself so solid that if I got hit by a car, the car would be smashed but I would be fine. I never tested my idea, but I believed it might be so.

Of course, along the way reality sets in. Struggling against that cement block, I almost didn't succeed. I came ever so close to losing--I was right at the edge. If the water had been a foot deeper, the block a pound heavier, I would have been forced to drop it and quit—to give up. I didn't consciously realize it, but that mix of concrete, muddy water and gravity had informed me of my limits.

I guess the kid in me wasn't ready for that. It scared me, and I didn't want to know.

Dropoff

The next year I had a good week at Stambaugh summer camp. I stayed away from Lifesaving, but enjoyed free swims, exploring the camp and sending Morse code with semaphore flags. The last evening at camp was special. Following supper, all scouts--a dozen troops strong from throughout Mahoning Valley-- assembled on the parade grounds by the lake. It was a colorful sight--troops and patrols lined up across the green lawn, everyone in smart uniform, decked out in merit badges, official patches, special awards and bright red neckerchiefs. The American flag and Boy Scout banners waved in the wind, high overhead at the front of our formations, and the brassy metal of the bugler's horn glinted against the summer-green forest backdrop. All that remained before the final playing of taps and lowering of flags was the ceremony for Order of the Arrow.

That week in camp, members of each troop had voted for two of their group for induction into the Order. The voting was secret ballot; the tapping out ceremony that evening would reveal the winners.

The commanding scout ordered all troops to attention. Then two senior scouts, themselves members of the Order, came forward. They were dressed as Indians, in headdress and war paint, buckskin and beads, feathers and moccasins. In silence, the Indians began their solemn ceremonial walk, passing along the rows of scouts. Now and then they stopped and turned to face a chosen scout. The biggest Indian raised his outstretched arm high overhead, and then swung it down hard on the shoulder of the elected scout. Three times the Indian raised his arm then struck down on the scout's shoulder. When the first Indian was done, the second placed upon the chosen scout a red necklace with a single, large white feather and two small blue beads. Then the Indians stepped back, turned and continued their silent walk.

When they came to Troop 25 and walked beside me, the Indians stopped and turned. I recognized one of them as our troop leader. He raised his arm, and when he clapped down hard on my shoulder I buckled and almost lost my balance—he almost knocked me over! When he did it a second time, I was ready, tensed all my muscles and drew up my shoulder to meet his force. I still caved some with his smack, but not nearly as bad. I fended off the third hit the same way. When they placed the feather necklace on me and turned to walk on, I was embarrassed about the first hit, but proud.

Being chosen by the troop and tapped in the ceremony was only the beginning. The real Order of the Arrow challenge would be the initiation, the ordeal, which would come a month later. I worried about it, that I wouldn't be good enough. They tried to keep ordeal tests secret, but most scouts knew there was a vow of silence, something about boiling water, and a dropoff--where you had to spend the night alone in the woods sleeping in a designated spot. I wasn't concerned about being alone at night, but I had heard persistent tales about guys dropped off in stagnant swamps full of muck, where the snakes started moving when the sun set. So when I arrived at Stambaugh Friday evening a month later for the ordeal, true to the motto "Be Prepared," I was ready with a pack full of gear. I had my pocketknife and Boy Scout hatchet, my sleeping bag and heavy air mattress, a warm blanket and flashlight and ground cloth and plenty of extra clothes.

There were about a dozen of us from the summer tapping ceremony. Everyone put up a good front, but you could tell most of us were anxious. A couple adult scoutmasters and several OA scouts would conduct the initiation. It started off easy with a meeting. We were told to maintain silence over the next twenty-four hours, and to use that time to reflect upon what scouting was all about—the Oath, the Law, the responsibilities and honor. I had never been quiet that long, but it seemed like keeping quiet wouldn't be hard. And it would be easy to think about scout pledges and values. We'd be allowed meals during the ordeal— they weren't going to starve us—but the portions would be smaller than usual. I guessed that was like a religious fast to make things more solemn. But I knew meals wouldn't be a problem, either. Then silence was imposed, and the ordeal began.

During our light supper, I began to realize you had to stay alert to keep from saying anything. Otherwise, without thinking, you might just blurt out "Please pass the milk." Silence was going to need more concentration than I first thought.

Following supper, we were led across the parade grounds and into the woods to an area reserved for large bonfires during summer camp days. Here we had our first real test. Each inductee was given two matches, a paper Dixie cup, an egg, a pinch of salt, and a pint of water and told to hard boil the egg. I knew where to start—getting a small fire going with matches was easy. But beyond that step, I was lost. I guessed you needed to boil the water in the cup somehow, but I didn't know how to keep the paper from burning. Looking at the fires of others nearby, the emerging consensus seemed to be that if you filled the cup with water and put it in the fire you might be able to get the water hot enough to cook the egg before the cup burned. So I tried that. But the water only warmed before the top edges of the cup became singed and burned and I began losing water. My egg hardly warmed at all before most of the water was lost, dousing my fire. No hard-boiled egg here. I felt dumb. I think a couple guys got it—that putting the salt in the water could alter the boiling point and somehow keep the cup from burning. But I wasn't one of them.

By then, night had fallen and it was time for the dropoff. The leaders instructed us to gather our gear and line up single file. All my dropoff preparations were dashed when they added, "No packs allowed." You could take only what you could carry in your arms. So I stretched my arms around my sleeping bag and as much of my stuff as I could manage. Others didn't have half the gear I did. Then the OA leader led us off into the woods. We hiked a long way, and my arms tired. Then the end of my extra blanket worked loose and started dragging. It caught on a bush and was pulled loose to the ground. I bent over to gather it up and dropped my sleeping bag. I struggled to pick everything up and get back in line. A little farther, when my dragging blanket snagged a second time, the scout behind me paused to pick it up and then carried it for me. By then my arms ached. I wondered when we would get to the swamp.

We were walking along a hillside when the leaders began tapping inductees on the shoulder and pointing to spots on the ground beside the path—your place for the night. These guys were lucky—they were on a hill. Every couple minutes someone else was tapped, and our line shortened. My arms were giving out and I knew the swamp must be just ahead when I felt a tap from behind. A leader pointed at an opening beside small bushes—on high ground! The scout behind me tossed my blanket when he walked past and disappeared into the night with the dwindling line.

I couldn't have asked for a better spot! It was open, flat and dry, sheltered under some trees. I rested my arms a few minutes. Then I cleared away sticks and old branches on the ground, put down my ground cloth, blew up my air mattress, unrolled the sleeping bag and spread my blanket over top. No fires were permitted on the dropoff, but I wouldn't need one. The early fall night was comfortably cool. I wished I hadn't lugged along all those extra clothes that I now didn't need. I slept pretty well that night.

In the morning I was pleased with myself as I sat atop my rolled up sleeping bag. I had made it through the night OK--I had met the dropoff test. And of course with no one around, I hadn't said anything to break the silence vow. I waited for the column to return along the path, so I could rejoin on the trek down the hill to breakfast. I had been able to consolidate most of my gear inside my sleeping bag so I could carry it better.

The morning birds were singing loudly when the group came along. I quietly picked up my stuff and fell in line. A couple minutes later when we came to the next dropoff site, the scout there picked up his sole possession, a sleeping bag, and joined us. As I walked past his spot I noticed he had made a cushion of green pine branches and soft needles to sleep on. He probably cut them from the nearby white pine. The cushion of pine kept him off the damp ground and gave him comfort. I thought about my ground cloth, air mattress and armful of heavy gear. His version of "Be Prepared" seemed clearly superior to mine. Maybe I hadn't done so well on the dropoff test, after all.

The OA ritual called for inductees to spend the day working together outdoors on a camp improvement project, like clearing brush or removing a fallen tree from a pathway—the kind of activity I enjoyed. So the morning went well gathering up rocks from a small field and stacking them into a central pile. But that Saturday the Mahoning Valley Council, the authority for all area Boy Scouts, had coincidentally arranged for a special scout matinee movie at the State Theater in downtown Youngstown. Hundreds of scouts from the county would be attending, and we were told we would be going, too. A big movie theater in downtown Youngstown didn't seem the right place for a vow of silence and high-minded reflection, but that was that. After lunch we boarded a camp bus and headed off to the movies.

The theater was packed full of noisy scouts. So far I had been able to stay silent. I was pleasantly surprised to find how easy it was to keep quiet in the middle of a yakking crowd—just to tune everything out and keep my mouth shut. Our little group followed our OA leader through the bustle in the theater entranceway and then up the stairway to the balcony. We sat together, off to one side, with a commanding view of the mass of fidgeting scouts below. Finally the movie started and the noise level subsided.

The movie was disappointing—I don't even recall what it was about--and when it ended the noise resumed. We stood up and waited our turn to file out of the balcony and back down the stairway. At the top of the stairs, one of the Order leaders stood beside a restroom door and pointed us in. I entered, walked up to a closed door on one of the stalls and knocked. "Anybody in there?" I asked. Instantly I realized it! "No, NO!! How could I have done that!?!" My mind raced ... "The one test I was passing ... I blew it! GEEZ OH MAN!!!" I thought, "... and of all places, here in a stupid bathroom!!" I was ashamed, angry at my stupidity. I broke the vow, and there was nothing I could do about it.

I rode the bus back to camp, dejected. I didn't know if others had heard me or not. But that didn't matter. My ordeal was over. I couldn't concentrate any more on the Oath and the Laws, and all those uplifting themes of scouting. So maybe a scout was supposed to be courteous. But I had failed my ordeal, politely knocking on a bathroom door.

Following supper in the mess hall, the two adult scoutmasters pronounced the initiation complete and startled me by welcoming all of us as new members of the Order. We talked about the tests, about how to boil the egg, and a little bit about the dropoff. When one scoutmaster asked how many had slipped up and talked during the vow of silence, I raised my hand and was surprised to see many others do the same. That made me feel better, knowing I wasn't the only one. But it didn't make me feel OK.

I appreciated what the scoutmasters explained to us about the ordeal, about the significance of going through the initiation. For them the ordeal wasn't about whether you had succeeded at each test. Instead it was the trying that was the most important thing, the thing that mattered. Maybe they were right. After all, they were grownups with families, and they knew you didn't always succeed at what you set out to do. The scoutmasters were on our side. But by then perhaps I had spent too much time in school, where everything you did was measured and graded, and you either passed or failed. Maybe too much time in baseball where you either won or you lost … In school it wasn't the trying that was most important, it was getting it right. In scouts there was a different kind of ruler, a more forgiving measuring stick than the one used in school.

So after that I was proud to wear my Order of the Arrow feather at Thursday troop meetings. But underneath that pride, lurking like a cold reptile somewhere in a darkened swamp, the memory wouldn't go away--a nagging feeling that I fell short, that I hadn't really measured up to the ordeal.

About a year later I dropped out of scouts. I explained to the scoutmaster that school work and sports were taking too much time for me to continue. There was some truth in that. But it wasn't the whole story.

VII

An overlay forms, of contours, hills and depressions, and the slopes evolve and lead us on. Uplands flow to ridges, and lowlands rise to meet ridges that push to ranges. The flow of our lands takes hold, compels, and we follow. Some landforms loom high. They may cast long shadow that bends movement away, or reflect strong light that attracts. We frequent valley, traverse high plains and pause before steep ranges.

Our movement conforms, and our passage becomes but an echo of the land we cross.

Freshman

Ninth grade ushered in a strain of respectability which 7th and 8th grades lacked. No longer a "junior" role—now we were part of the real high school. Now we had a name to go with the grade number ... freshman.

Freshman level classes were a clear step upward to the next rung. Simple math was replaced with Algebra—the word, itself, sounded serious. Plain, ordinary numbers weren't enough anymore—now we would learn to prod at X's to decipher their inner nature, solve equations with multiple variables, and define that which was previously unknown. Those calculated feats would be a far cry from silently repeating "A Rat In The House Might Eat The Ice Cream" so you could spell "arithmetic" correctly at the top of your third grade quiz paper.

The stink of formaldehyde jars in Mr. Weiss' Biology class was much worse than those smelly paste jars in grade school. With Biology, childish ways of double hooking night crawlers on your fishing hook and stalking bullfrogs at water's edge with a BB gun were put aside. And what a few years earlier was considered cruelty by a kid using a pocketknife now became a course requirement with a dissection knife. Slitting animals was now deemed educational and justified with the scientific labeling of carved pieces of those creatures—cerebral ganglia ... tympanic membrane. Seeing a rabbit's heart beat and learning that frog innards resembled the insides of people seemed important. But those lessons required Greg, Warren, Barbara, Jack and I to check squeamish feelings at the classroom door. Fortunately, Mr. Weiss appreciated those feelings, and he tempered cut and dry academics with a little blood and guts human understanding on dissection days.

Latin with Mrs. Hitchcock stood quietly amid freshman classes, a lone column of ancient knowledge. It lacked the mystery of Algebra and the odors of Biology, but its permanence and deep overlay of rules inspired trust. It was an ageless, solid subject you could count on—many English words were founded on a Latin base. Verb conjugations and pronoun declensions could be hard to memorize. But you could turn some into rhythmic, football-like cheers ... "Hic Haec Hoc! Huius Huius Huius!" or "Sui Sibi Se Se!" The chants helped. Translations were challenging. But with a little help from patient Mrs. Hitchcock, pulling apart phrases and sorting out word endings, Latin always made sense in the end. Translating Latin might confuse you, but it would never trick you. It always followed the rules.

Entering the bus at the end of the day, an armful of homework, Latin, Biology and Algebra texts stacked atop your three-ring binder slung against your hip, a serious freshman always impressed younger riders.

Freshman Football

As freshmen, our class produced its first team. Now there were team uniforms, chalked fields, bleachers with fans, a coach and cheerleaders—elements missing from our neighborhood football games on Kaufel's field.   Little League and Pony League had contributed some of those distinguishing elements of organized sport, but baseball encompassed only your immediate team. With freshman football, the notion of team broadened to embrace the whole freshman class.

The change didn't take hold overnight—classmates didn't flock to the stands, like a swooping rush of blackbirds to the cornfield across from Kaufel's. Attendance at freshman football games was spotty, most of the bleachers empty. But through the season a nucleus was forming, as that same gaggle of 6th grade kids in quirky costumes from Over the Rainbow, the same pack of guys under floppy shoulder pads and wobbly plastic helmets of neighborhood scrimmages began to move in more uniform procession along the yellow bricks.

Football hurt. There wasn't anything easy about it. It was serious, and it commanded submission.

When I began playing football for the Canfield Cardinals I weighed about 130 pounds. So I got a barbell and weights and began working out religiously three times a week, trying to put on weight. After four years of working out, by senior year, I had bulked up to 142. I grew stronger during that time, but no matter how hard I worked, my body wouldn't get any bigger. Because of my size, I figured I just had to try harder.

Football meant commitment to daily practice. Summer practice was the toughest. As each new school year approached, August 20th signaled the end of summer and the start of two-a-day practices—one in the morning, the second that afternoon. The coaches knew we had only about two weeks to prepare for the first game in September, so they pushed hard.

Come the 20th, it was up early and off to practice. In the locker room you suited up with full pads—there was no easing into it. That first day everything you put on was clean. But thereafter, morning socks, shoulder pads and T shirts were smelly sweaty from the day before. The practice field was behind the school, adjacent to the varsity game field. Workouts began around 8 with jumping jacks, pushups, stretching and calisthenics, followed by a series of agility, reaction, blocking, tackling and conditioning drills. By then the sun had begun to beat down, and you could expect morning temperatures to rise into the 80's. Then the team broke into smaller groups for more drills and practice based on your position on offense, followed by defensive drills. Then we reassembled into offense and defense squads to practice new plays you had studied in your playbook the previous night. And during all the drills and activities, you kept moving, constantly on the go, bellowing and shouting and cheering team mates on, because a football team doesn't get into shape just standing around. Morning practice ended with a series of wind sprints, back and forth and back and forth across the practice field, the hard running meant to leave you bent over, hands on knees, huffing and puffing.

We had an hour off for lunch. Off came helmets, jerseys, T shirts and shoulder pads. We sunned on the grass and lounged on grade school playground equipment near the locker room, subdued, eating lunches brought from home. The best part was always the quart container of cold orange juice Mom had packed. An hour was just about enough time to nurse your wounds, replenish fluids, and prepare to do it again.

Afternoon practice was like morning practice, except you were already beat, that morning blister on your foot now tore open, the rubbing on your neck from too-tight shoulder pads really started to wear away the skin, and always it was hotter. On days when temperatures hit the 90's, the trainer passed out salt pills, which were supposed to help--no one keeled over, so maybe they did. Through it all you kept summoning forth from somewhere the intensity to keep at it, drill after drill. Two or three hours later, as you stood catching your breath from the last wind sprint, you could finally head back to the locker room, shower and go home. Most evenings it hurt just to move. So you'd eat dinner, study new plays and go to bed early. Tomorrow, you would do it all again.

After a couple weeks the two-a-days stopped with the start of classes, and practice subsided to a more tolerable single session after school.

Mr. Weiss from Biology doubled as freshman football coach. On the first day of practice, I tackled someone in a drill, hitting him low and wrapping up his knees, as I had learned to do in neighborhood games on Meadowview. As I got up, Coach Weiss smiled and said my form was "tremendous." I appreciated his compliment. But we freshmen would be only a mediocre team. Effort, commitment and form would prove to be important ingredients in football that season—they all mattered. But to win you also had to be good.

It was an after-school game late freshman season. We had won a few games, but losses outnumbered the wins. Behind the school, a small crowd of freshmen in the stands and parents scattered along the sidelines watched as Canfield freshmen battled the visitors. The air was chilly, and most of the leaves on the maples behind the south end zone were down—fall was about over. As the fourth quarter drew to a close, Nancy, Kathy and the rest of the freshman cheerleaders were doing their best, urging on a couple dozen of the class faithful in the bleachers … "Come on boys, you can do it! Yeah man, yes you can!"

Canfield was behind by a couple points, and the game was almost finished. The clock was stopped with only a few seconds left to tick off—enough time for one more play. Our defense had just held the visitors on 3rd down to force a punt, and I went back to receive the kick. As I stood there waiting for the ref to blow his whistle and resume play, I realized, "If I can run this punt back, we'll win." I had never scored a touchdown or made a big play in any of our games. But now, here was a chance. The game was on the line.

I thought about that chance, and tried to reach down inside to find some untapped level of resolve and strength. I focused all my thought as hard as I could, and said to myself—"I can DO it! I can DO IT!!" I was determined. I looked up field to the two teams lining up for the punt, and beyond the line of scrimmage to the end zone by the maples. That's where I needed to go. "I can do it!" I told myself again. Nothing was going to stop me. Mind and body were committed.

It was a good punt, and I moved under it and caught it. I looked up to see a lone defender coming at me fast getting close, with the rest of them still up field. I faked a move one way and cut back to lose the first guy. He lost his balance and went down in front of me. I leaped up to hurdle him, looking to the next wave up field. But in mid air my foot caught his shoulder, I went tumbling and down I came, thud on the field.

The ref blew his whistle, and the play was dead. The game was over. I hadn't even made it past the first guy. And the loss column ticked up one more notch on Canfield's losing season record.

To be sure, effort, commitment and form were important ingredients in the contest—they all mattered. But to win at football, you also had to be good enough to keep conviction from tripping over reality.

Erie Local

Room 220 Study Hall was in the high school section, up on the second floor. Opposite the hall entrance were several tall windows stretching to the high ceiling and looking out the backside of the school, over the slide, teeter-totters, and swings of the grade school playground, across the football field and past the open bleachers to the houses along Edwards Avenue. On sunny fall days, the lower windows were tilted open to keep the room cool. And a light rush of breeze carried in the afternoon noise of the town—the creaking of metal swings in the soft breeze, insistent chatter of robins in the maples along the edge of the playground, and occasional growling semis leaving the village, heading west on Route 224, their flatbeds heavy with thick slabs and coil steel from the mills around Youngstown.

Study hall was just that—a room to study--no talking permitted. The teacher's desk stood up front on a raised wooden platform, about a foot above the floor. From there the teacher had a commanding view to ensure students kept eyes trained where they belonged—down into textbooks. So each 5th period I sat in 220 and focused my vision where I was supposed to. But while my eyes were aimed at Biology and Algebra, my 5th period ears were tuned elsewhere, to the sounds drifting in through the windows from past the playground, over the football field, and beyond the houses on Edwards. And somewhere into the hour, I'd jerk when I heard the train whistle.

By 9th grade, I knew that whistle was the Erie freight working his way south. He had left Niles about an hour earlier and was heading down the Lisbon Branch with a short train. From the tone of the horn, I knew two old Alco diesel engines were lugging the train--a handful of boxcars and gondolas on the head end, followed by about fifteen empty coal hoppers and a tired red caboose. This was the lone train on the branch that dropped south from the Erie mainline at Niles, served Canfield, worked into the farms and low hills south of town, crossed the busy mainline of the Pennsylvania Railroad ten miles south at Leetonia, and then wandered deep into the hills of Columbiana County to the coal tipple at Lisbon.

From first grade onward, each afternoon at school I heard the Erie blow for the crossing at 224, followed by low rumblings that diminished as the train crossed the highway and pulled alongside the wood frame station and stopped. I knew the agent would walk out onto the station platform, the train crew would climb down from the locomotive, and the conductor might walk forward from the caboose. They would nod hello's, sort through a few waybills of the day's business, discuss the B&O boxcar of dimensional lumber to be placed at the shed in the lumber yard, the Rock Island boxcar of burlap-bagged seed corn to be spotted at Delf's & Sons, and the Lackawanna coal hopper to be shoved up onto the trestle for unloading. Then the trainmen would return to the engine, and the crew would work the sidings, pulling and pushing the freight cars into place. I knew in about twenty minutes, the work done, the local would resume the trip south. It was a slow operation, never much more than 15 or 20 miles an hour.

So when I heard that whistle come floating through the study hall windows, a kind of metallic bleating, I knew the train had crossed Herbert Road about five minutes earlier and the engineer was now approaching the flashing lights at Route 224, a little beyond those houses on Edwards Avenue.

For years I had listened from inside the school to the daily arrival of that train. But until freshman year, I had never been in a classroom where I might see it. I was always enclosed in the front of the school, or down on the first floor, or my classroom had no windows opening to the west. So when I landed in 220 early afternoons freshman year, I was optimistic. Maybe, finally, I could catch some glimpse of that train … maybe the top of a boxcar just over the roof of one of those white houses on Edwards, or some dark movement of rusty freight cars through the clump of trees beyond the football goal posts. Or if I looked just right, maybe I could spot the roof of the engine cab as it came to a stop near the station, at the top of the rise.

So that semester I studied my narrow band of landscape out the windows to the west. Each week I became more adept at disguising my gazing beyond Edwards as merely a brief, casual glance. It wasn't hard—it just required a cautious, gradual approach. I didn't get caught—the teacher never asked what I was looking at or told me to get back to work.

137

But I failed. Try as I might, no matter how thoroughly I scanned the roofs and the treetops, or which gap between the houses I considered, or how intently I peered through blowing branches and leaves, I never spotted that train. As the semester wore on, I finally brought myself to concede the railroad was too far away, hidden from my daily view. No matter how clearly the local freight called, the train was tucked just over the horizon.

Sitting in study hall, I could only listen as the engineer, his work in town now done, would slowly notch up the throttle, the diesels would churn and strain against the freight cars, and the Erie would begin moving south again, blowing first for the crossing on Lisbon Street. The string of empty hoppers would slow click-clack ... click-clack over worn rail as the train resumed its labored march. The caboose would rock and lean as it ground slowly past the station, picking up the pace, leaving Delf's behind. Shortly he'd blow again for the bypass near the fairgrounds, moving in a rhythmic clanking and swaying, now a steady gait on his way out of town. Off again southbound, following his daily rounds ... Over the next few minutes the clacking and clanking of the distant freight would gradually soften, the rumblings slowly taper off, and the sounds of the train would blend back into the light rush of breeze through open window, the creaking of playground swings, the tranquility of the quiet afternoon, and be lost.

Sophomore

Sophomore football players practiced with the varsity. We weren't on the actual varsity—most sophomores and a handful of juniors were relegated to the second tier, the Junior Varsity. At practice, coaches worked with JV players the same as varsity players to improve skills and technique, since coaches recognized JV's would become varsity players in a year or two. But true varsity players regarded sophomores only half seriously, for they understood the fundamental role of JV's--cannon fodder for juniors and seniors.

The varsity offense practiced their plays against our JV defense. I played safety. On pass plays, I'd try to cover the receiver, and on runs varsity linemen blocked the hole and then came downfield to take out safeties. Victories on the practice field were few for us

JV's. Occasionally we'd break up a pass or avoid a hit from a lineman. Whenever a small success like that happened, the coaches shouted encouragement at the varsity player, usually ignoring what the JV had done well. By mid season, most of the grass on the practice field was beaten down to big patches of dry dirt. And our white practice uniforms of August were now beige and brown, ground with layers of sweat stains and smears of earth. For Roger, Larry, Pete, Richy and the rest of us sophomores, being a JV was a drab, dusty, thankless job.

One day as the end of the season neared, the high school was assembled in the auditorium for a football pep rally. Freshman and sophomore classes were seated in the bleachers, and juniors and seniors were in chairs on the main floor. Varsity cheerleaders, dressed in bright red and white outfits, led the school in cheers and shouts, and Coach Peterson and a couple seniors said a few words to the student body about Canfield's upcoming game. Then Coach Reinhart walked to the front of the auditorium beside a large blackboard he had positioned there. In practice, we frequently used that board to diagram plays.

"James, front and center," Coach Reinhart ordered. James was a senior lineman—the biggest guy on the team. In addition to football, he was on Student Council--everyone at school knew him. James got up from his seat and walked forward.

"Gentzel, front and center," the Coach called out. The Coach was looking into the bleachers at me. I didn't know what was going on, but when the Coach said move, you moved. I stood and worked my way between classmates along the bleachers, then out the rear door and downstairs, and finally back through the side door into the auditorium.   James and the coach were waiting beside the blackboard.   Coach Reinhart motioned for me to stand beside James, facing everyone. James was about a foot taller and a hundred pounds heavier. Students smiled at the contrast.

I was nervous, so I didn't catch everything the Coach first said. I heard some things about students knowing James, and cheering for upperclassmen at games. He motioned at me and talked about underclassmen and the JV squad that no one notices. Then the Coach picked up some chalk and turned to his blackboard. He drew an offensive formation set against a defense.

139

"So, every day at practice," the Coach began, "James and the varsity line up against the JV defense. James is at tackle." And Reinhart made a couple heavy circles to accent James' left tackle position on the board. "And Gentzel is back here at safety." And he drew a heavy circle on my safety position.

"Now, every snap, James has two assignments. First is to block the defensive man over him." And the Coach drew a couple lines showing James blocking the tackle across from him. "And once he hits the lineman, James' next assignment is …" and Reinhart turned back to the board and marked a path for James straight at the safety, "… Get Gentzel." And with a flourish, Reinhart chalked a big X over my position. People laughed.

"Now, when James executes that assignment and takes out Gentzel, when he gets back to the huddle, he hears 'Good job, James!'" Then he paused, for effect … "And Gentzel … he doesn't hear a thing." More laughs.

James and I were smiling along, too. Then Coach Reinhart turned serious and proceeded with his real message--how obscure JV's, lowly sophomores, worked every day at practice, taking those hits with no fanfare, notice or thanks. The Coach wanted students to recognize the contribution which JV's were making to help varsity players become better, to help the school win. Then the Coach asked all the JV's to stand to the applause of the student body. He finally dismissed James and me to return to our seats.

It was a good pep talk. Students and players got the message. Later at practice, all of us JV's were fired up and eager for the opportunity to knock heads with the varsity.

Coach Reinhart was solid, but he wasn't a big man—he wasn't much taller than I was. Thinking now about his message, I suspect that pep rally wasn't the first time he considered the role of small players on a big team. Somewhere back in his high school days, long before I was around, I imagine he had learned something about dusty practice fields and being a tackling dummy for seniors. That lesson must have left its mark as he grew up, went out into the world and years later came to Canfield to help coach.

When Coach Reinhart addressed students at the pep rally that day, outside our school building the breezes were soft. Inside the auditorium the air was still. But as he stood before the student body, next to his chalk board and spoke, a quiet wind somewhere stirred, and a light dusting from the Coach's old high school practice field kicked up and blew across the years to color that Canfield pep rally.

Leetonia

May and early June were the toughest weeks at school—the pressure of semester tests, due dates for book reports and term paper deadlines. To make matters worse, spring fever set in about then, making it especially hard to buckle down and study those last few weeks. So with the onset of May, I needed something positive out there, the prospect of a reward beyond that last day of school, something to help me stay focused the rest of the semester and push through to summer vacation. And so was born my annual summer pilgrimage to Leetonia.

Back in junior high, a Sunday edition of the <u>Youngstown Vindicator</u> included an article about a Civil War locomotive traveling the US as part of the Centennial. That day The General was to depart from Lisbon on the Erie branch and steam into Leetonia, the potato chip factory town where I had seen trains years before. Mom and Dad agreed to go for a Sunday drive to see the engine, and so the family loaded up and headed off to Franklin Square, a rural crossing on the Erie branch, a couple miles south of Leetonia.

When we arrived, a few people were already there, standing in the weeds trackside. We joined them, milling around, waiting and listening. The branch headed off into the woods, forming an alleyway into the forest. In a little while, distant chugging arose from the woods. A minute later, white smoke rose over the trees down the right of way, a headlight appeared, and the bright red engine came into view, puffing along toward the crossing. It approached at a measured pace, as the train grew closer and bigger under steady puffing. Our little crowd stepped back as the train neared the crossing, and the whistle shrieked as the engine passed—black, shiny brass and bright red cab. A yellow passenger car clumped along behind.

We quickly returned to the car and Dad headed north. We watched from afar the rhythmic turning of the big engine wheels as the bright engine puffed along through the trees and the lowlands,

141

toward the junction at Leetonia. As the little train drew alongside the mainline and eased up to the signal at the junction, a long westbound Pennsylvania Railroad freight rolled through town behind three black diesels. Each had a shiny red PRR keystone on its side. The fireman on the freight spotted the old steam engine, and he leaned far out his cab window to study the little locomotive as his freight rolled by on the main. The two trains whistled greetings as they passed, and I thought, "This would be a good place to watch trains."

Dad had brought home a worn leather briefcase from somewhere at work. A couple pockets and flaps of the old leather were so dry and brittle they easily tore and crumbled. But most of the case was still solid. With wire and coat hangers, I rigged the briefcase to the frame and chain guard at the rear wheel of my Columbia bike, saddlebag style. The night before my pilgrimage, I packed the case with Boy Scout canteen of water, pens and notepads for train notes, and a couple Crescent wrenches I borrowed from Dad in case the bike needed adjustment along the way. In the kitchen, I packed a sandwich, orange and a stack of Oreo's in a brown paper bag and put it in the refrigerator.

The next morning, the alarm rang before sunup--get dressed, eat a quick breakfast, transfer lunch from refrigerator to briefcase--and I was ready. Mom and Dad were just getting up, and on my way out the door Mom reminded me, "We'll pick you up by the tower tonight at 8 o'clock. Be careful, now—make sure you watch out for cars." Twice I had talked friends into pedaling along with me—once Jack and another time Fred--but usually I went alone. Carol and Nancy were still in bed, enjoying the chance to sleep in with the start of summer vacation. With first light, I was on my way.

It wasn't a race. But the faster I pedaled, the sooner I'd get there. My Columbia had big balloon tires and no gears. It wasn't built for speed, but at only 24 inches the bike was light, so I managed to keep a good pace. Traffic was sparse at that hour, and passing cars gave me a wide space at the side of the road. Along Raccoon I negotiated a few little ups and downs as I passed scattered houses and then Skelton's farm at the crossroads. The mile along Shields was flat, and the fresh morning air spurred me on. From the top of the ridge at the corner of Shields and 46, I could look to the west, overtop the turnpike cut into the ridge below, past the S curve in Herbert Road, beyond the distant willow rising over the pond by the old folks home, and spot a stretch of the Erie branch where it cut across the corn fields about a mile away, heading south toward Canfield. I turned left onto 46. From that point I'd be paralleling the Erie route the next eleven miles, all the way to Leetonia.

Route 46 was a two-lane highway, with moderate car traffic and occasional trucks. The highway was wider than country roads. Early morning traffic was light, and the stretch from Shields south into Canfield was mostly downhill—clear sailing. About twenty-five minutes from home, I crested the knoll near the Parkview at the north end of the green and came pedaling into town.

The village was waking up. At Main and Broad, gas station attendants were lifting open their garage doors; the pumps were ready. Across the way Islay's would soon be opening. Robins were searching the green for worms, and a few sparrows poked at the dirt around the park benches near the Methodist Church. Beyond the green, the rest of the town was just beginning to stir—it had yet to start the day. I stopped for the traffic light on 224, and then resumed pedaling when it changed green, leaving behind the locked doors of Farmers Bank and the Five and Ten, past McCabe Drug and the library, and out the south end of the square.

At the edge of town, I rolled past Knight's Restaurant, a little roadside cafe—still closed at that hour--and came to the fairgrounds. Here the bypass from 224 joined 46, and the Erie branch came into full view a quarter mile off to the right. It cut through the fields and skirted an orchard at the Mahoning County experimental farm. The sun had started its climb, and morning dew was now beginning to burn off. With early June the corn in the County fields was up and making a strong push toward "knee high by the 4th."

I kept to the gravel along the shoulder of 46. The traffic moved faster along this stretch, and the coal trucks heading to the strip mines in Columbiana County on their first run of the day didn't yield any room as they charged south. Past Leffingwell and then the turkey farm on the right, the Erie branch followed at a distance.

At Western Reserve, I jogged a few hundred yards to the west to pick up the county road to Washingtonville just before the old wooden crossbuck at the Erie crossing. The Erie once called the place Marquis—it was a station stop at one time. No structures remained, and the place was now but a spur off the branch in a secluded clump of trees. The rickety spur headed east, up an easy grade about a half mile to a clay company. Usually the spur track was empty. But if yesterday's local had set off a gondola or a bad order coal hopper, I'd park my bike in the weeds, walk the uneven ties, and climb up the end ladders of the cars to inspect them. The steel rungs were still cool from the night air, and the wet sides of the freight cars slow dripped dew into the weeds and overgrown ties. The freight cars were usually empty, and the massive interior of the hard steel walls and angled slope sheets seemed out of place amid surrounding leaves and fresh vegetation. After I climbed down, it was hard to wipe the rusty residue off my hands.

The stretch from Western Reserve to Washingtonville was the best part of the ride. The road cut straight south over open green fields, farmland and apple orchards. The pavement was narrow, but the surface smooth. Infrequent cars and pickups gave me wide berth as each passed in a hard whoosh of wind and humming tires. And the road reached south for miles in long gentle slopes. Redwing blackbirds sang my journey along from their fence posts, past little crossroads under shade trees, past Calla, Greenford and, in one corner of a field, an empty red brick school building from an earlier time. My pedaling spun a steady rhythm into the new day, and all along the way, just over the rise to the west, the Erie branch wandered south under blue skies toward Leetonia.

At Washingtonville, the track swung in from a quarry and came alongside the road. Track and road skirted a low stone wall and shaded cemetery for a half block before they crossed route 14. Washingtonville was a one street town, with a stretch of small buildings and houses along 14 as the road came down a long grade. The crossing was at the bottom of the hill, protected with red flashing lights. The lights were dark—the Erie local wouldn't set them blinking until it eased into town much later that afternoon.

144

A block south of 14, the railroad crossed my road and headed left, off into the trees on the last mile into Leetonia. The road to Leetonia jogged right and then turned south again, confronting Leetonia Hill. At the base of the hill, an abandoned railroad right of way curved in from the west. At one time tracks had extended five miles to Salem, but the rail was torn up decades before, and all that remained was a narrow path which trees and bushes were retaking. My road took the hill head on, and I pedaled fast to get a running start. The incline was long and steep--I could make it only half way before my legs gave out and I had to get off and walk the bike the rest of the way.

By the top of the grade, I had caught my breath and was ready for the home stretch. Entering Leetonia just past the hilltop, I veered left onto Walnut Street, and from there it was all downhill. Past the high school and quiet football field on the left, past a couple open blocks of city park, coasting by big Victorian houses, then braking the final blocks down the hillside, past old, two-story brick offices and stores near Main Street. At the base of the hill, Walnut opened to the railroad junction. There I stopped.

The mainline of the Pennsylvania Railroad entered town on a sweeping curve from the left. The eastbound and the westbound main tracks were laid with heavy rail and ties on deep ballast. The tops of the rails were polished smooth by the passing of trains. Flashing lights and crossing gates protected Walnut and another street at the base of the hill. The curve from the east tapered off near Walnut, and the two tracks then headed west out of town on a mile-long straightaway.

The single track of the Erie branch also curved in from the left, emerging from behind Leetonia Hill and bending up against the Pennsylvania tracks. A small Erie freight station stood beside the branch, just east of Walnut. The locked depot was bounded behind by worn tracks and on the front side by a small parking area paved in bricks. Thick layers of white and green paint peeled from the wooden station, while grasses and dandelions sprouted between parking lot bricks. A grey PRR freight house stood opposite the Erie depot, on the far side of the mainline.

The Pennsylvania interlocking tower that guarded the junction rose beside the main tracks just west of Walnut. The two-story tower was rectangular, about ten by fifteen, painted the same gray as the freight house. Its roof sloped on all sides, and small radio antennas poked up on two wooden poles above roofline. The tower was manned around the clock, every day of the year, for the trains never stopped. A sturdy, wooden stairway ascended the backside to the second floor entrance. From up there, the operator controlled switches and trackside signals below where the Erie merged into the westbound main, crossed over to the eastbound in the shadow of the tower and then diverged again on the way out of town. To the west, the Erie branch paralleled the mainline tangent for a mile before it swung southwest toward Franklin Square.

It was just past 8 o'clock, the aroma of warm potato chips flavored the morning air, summer vacation was upon me, and over the next twelve hours I could count on a couple dozen trains coming through town. How could life get any better?

I spent the day at things only a railroad fan could appreciate. Mornings I poked around the tracks at the junction and followed the mainline bending through some curves to the east. I had read that a Youngstown & Southern branch once reached Leetonia from Columbiana, and I explored the mainline looking for remnants of abandoned tracks. Later in the morning I pedaled past the potato chip plant and then west about a half mile to the first crossing. In trees and brush along the north side of the tracks were concrete foundations of some forgotten industry, a series of square structures with crumbling walls several feet tall. Fifteen foot trees sprouted from within the old walls. Climbing over the remains, I guessed the railroad switched cars of clay or coal to those buildings years before. And throughout the day, every time a train came rolling into town, I dropped what I was doing, grabbed my notepad from the briefcase and recorded the time and direction of travel, the kind of train and locomotives, the railroad facts of its passing ... 9:07 am, westbound, F7 ABB and GP9, coal train, 82 cars ... 9:52 am, eastbound, 3 new U25B's, tructrain, 67 cars, 3 cabooses.

A strange kid hanging around the tracks--nosing through underbrush, scribbling notes in a briefcase—was something unusual

146

for Leetonia. I met with long stares from locals driving slowly over the crossings, from the attendant working the gas station on Columbia Street and the kid at the hamburger stand near the tracks. As I poked around east of the junction, across the tracks from the gas station, the gas station guy would lean the spare tire up against the frame of the garage door, study me for a few minutes, then turn and ask his buddy, "Just what do you suppose he's up to?"

His buddy would watch me for a minute, lift his ball cap at the greasy visor and scratch his forehead. "Well … I don't know. He must be up to something." Then they'd both look a little more before going back to work changing the tire.

People seldom stepped forward and asked me what I was doing— mostly they just liked to look. Maybe they enjoyed the mystery. On those rare occasions when someone did speak up, I'd answer that I was watching trains. From their reaction I saw my answer shed a little light on the matter for them, but it still didn't exactly explain things. But watching trains wasn't something you could easily explain. So I went about my business, ignoring the stares—I figured it just came with the territory.

By noon I had pedaled along the Pennsylvania tracks to the first curve west of town. Positioned on the outside of the curve, I could look right down that mile straightaway back to Leetonia, and to the left, down another mile of straight track through low woods and open field to another distant curve. A full two miles of mainline tracks lay stretched before me, and just behind me the Erie branch broke away toward Franklin Square. There in the middle of the countryside, a long way from the stares, I plopped my bike down in the weeds and ate lunch.

A summer grittiness clung to the railroad. The hot sun warmed the ties, forcing up an ooze of tars and creosote. The harsh smells mixed with the odor of soot and grime that countless passing trains had left behind as they roared through. Years of swirling diesel exhaust, brake shoe smoke, oily splatters and particles of steel scraped from flanges against rail had settled upon the tracks and worked deep into the ballast. The result was a roadbed covered in accumulations of blackened dirt and dust--it smudged the bottom of your shoes with dark marks water couldn't wash away. Here and there old spikes and tie plates littered the ballast. And beyond the rail and ballast, belched far outward trackside, was a deep layer of black cinders ejected by a hundred years of steam locomotives which had come that way. A tangle of grasses, weeds, Queen Ann's Lace and low crawling vines now grew upon the cinders and held the deposit firm to the ground. But you didn't have to kick down far at the roots to expose the dark layer and know what had come before.

Atop the summer grittiness, the trains moved in a shimmering. At the far end of the straightaway, just to the right of the tiny gray tower at the junction, the yellow lights of the eastbound home signal glimmered through the daylight. And the tops of the rails, shiny and polished in the midday sun, stretched like silver threads toward the distant junction. Way down the line, heat waves baked up, distorting the polish of the rails to a far away shimmer. Then I'd hear a faint horn from beyond the junction, a higher pitch than usual. It was 53, the Fort Pitt, the afternoon passenger train from Pittsburgh, and the high pitch meant he was coming fast. More horn blowing for the crossings in town, then he'd round the sweeping curve into Leetonia, slice past the tower and set his sights on my straightaway.

His tiny yellowish headlight reflected off polished rails, bent by the wavering heat. He sped up the line, a little roar growing louder, emerging from the waves, the headlight beaming more intense. Another high pitched whistle for the next crossing, as the train loomed larger and louder. Then the rail at the curve began to vibrate, to quiver, like it could feel the wheels of the fast train skimming toward it. And the noise and shaking grew as smooth diesels leaned into the curve, towered up then roared past. Weeds blew back and the ground shook, and long cars slammed by in quick succession. Bright stainless cars, a few heads whisked by behind the glare of windows, and in seconds it was past. The wind calmed and the rear red marker lights raced away down the next straightaway. The skimming steel faded softer, and the train receded into the distance. Smaller and smaller, 53 bore down on the vanishing point, and the tiny train gradually sank back into more heat waves.

Finally it turned into the far bend. Quietly, first the engines disappeared into the curve, then the express cars and in a few moments the last shimmering car silently slipped away behind the trees. And I picked up my notebook ... 1:32 pm #53 westbound, 2 E8 A's, 4 Railway Express cars, 3 passenger cars.

Afternoons I pushed farther west to the next curve, where 53 had slipped from view. Here steel girders carried the railroad across a low spot, over a lazy stream. The two tracks were spaced far apart on the bridge, separated by a wooden deck which a third main track once occupied. I walked my bike across the bridge on the middle wooden timbers, stepping carefully over the gaps opening to muddy water below. On the far side, you could sit for a long while, tossing stones and ballast rocks into the water below, disturbing the calm afternoon with hollow plops when they broke the water. And all the while, trains flowed back and forth across the landscape ... 2:47 pm eastbound TT-2, tructrain from Chicago, 3 GP35's 91 cars ... 3:12 pm, westbound, Baldwin sharknose ABB, mixed boxcar freight, 62 cars ... 3:36 pm, sound of Erie local going south ...

Sometimes I'd stash my bike in the trees and bushes near the tracks and climb away from the railroad, up the hill beyond the bridge. From a high, open field I could survey the little valley. Below the bridge, the stream meandered south, twisting across lowlands and pastures. Beyond the stream, a mile off to the right, two country roads led to the cluster of houses and trees at Franklin Square. Now and then a stray car crossed the lowland, winding along one of the roads into the Square. Only a stop sign marked the village intersection. Toward the east, bisecting the fields and valley landscape, the mainline angled away, leading straight and true from the girder bridge back toward the curve where I ate lunch. The railroad pole line, dozens of copper wires tying together the far reaches of the railroad, followed the south edge of the tracks. Low wooded hills on the north reached out to the inside of the distant curve. Across the full expanse, the land was fresh green against a strong blue sky. The earth smelled sweet with new growth. From somewhere off to the south, the distant, hollow barking of a dog wouldn't quit, and the sun warmed the afternoon air.

Later in the day I pedaled back to the junction. Supper was a burger, fries and a chocolate shake from the stand down the street from the gas station. Buying something in town usually softened the stares. Afterward I pedaled over to the interlocking tower and leaned my bike against the back wall by the steps. Then I clomped up the stairway to the second floor and knocked on the door.

"Yeah, come on in," came a shout from inside. I opened the door, ready to introduce myself and ask if I could spend some time in the tower, watching. When I stepped inside, the operator recognized me. It was Popeye, the regular second trick operator. Popeye lived in Leetonia and had worked towers on the division for years. He'd seen me poking around earlier that evening. There were company rules against visitors in the tower. But unlike everyone else in town, he understood what I was up to.

"Come on in," he repeated. He was seated at a worn desk at the opposite end of the room. "Close the door," he said as he tossed his paperback book into an open desk drawer and kicked the drawer shut. Popeye was lean, about forty, with dark features. He wore old slacks and a plain, open collar, short-sleeve shirt. "Haven't seen you for a while," he said.

I closed the door and walked toward his end of the room. Popeye presided over a vintage railroad world—scents of aged wood, old dust and fresh grease filled the air. A long bank of steel levers was aligned down the middle of the room. Each lever connected a switch or trackside signal below that directed trains through the junction. The chest-high levers were decades old, the handle grips polished with wear. The old mechanism was complex--electrical timers and lever releases interlocked with track switches and signals to prevent train wrecks. A long schematic diagram of the junction hung from the ceiling above the bank of levers, white track lines on a black background, with each of the switches and signals keyed to a lever. When Popeye grabbed a lever, squeezed the release and pushed the metal bar forward, the ancient mechanism moved and locked down with a smooth, solid clank.

"I guess it has been a while," I answered. Fresh air blew in through a screen window near Popeye's desk, the potato chip plant having shut down for the evening. "I was here for a few hours last fall once, but I don't think you were working that day. I didn't know the operator—I think he said he usually worked Youngstown and Girard."

"Yeah … that was probably Smitty," Popeye responded.

I leaned against the wall, beside an array of company bulletins, official railroad postings, orders from the Division Superintendent along with Work Safe posters tacked to the wooden wall. An old broom and dustpan leaned nearby—I think they were the same place last fall. "Is there anything coming?" I asked.

Popeye looked at his train sheet, a huge paper form that covered most of the desktop. "I've got a westbound—he's about a half hour away." Then he looked up at the big whiteface clock on the wall. "Twenty-two should be coming in about an hour." Then he added, "The Erie put a couple cars on the ground near Lisbon—he won't be back through tonight." We talked trains and a little baseball, and the quiet evening drifted in through the windows. Occasional cars on Walnut passed below, bumping cautiously over the tracks.

Popeye sat ringed in with phones and radios. The local Bell phone was pushed to one side of the desk—it was seldom used. Beside it, the railroad speaker phone extended on a retractable arm from the wall. It rang with a loud jangle, connecting Leetonia to other towers and stations along the railroad—that was Popeye's main communication line. A gray desktop speaker could radio crews of passing locomotives and cabooses, though reception on the train radio was temperamental. And a dark green metal box the size of a loaf of bread was screwed to a shelf over the desk. Four round lights across the front of the box, two for the eastbound track and two for the westbound, were wired to trackside signals about two miles either side of town—the round lights blinked off when an approaching train entered that stretch of track.

The phones were still, and the minute hand inched around the face of the wall clock. Our talk turned from the Cleveland Indians to high school football next fall, and Popeye unscrewed the lid from his stained thermos and poured himself some coffee. The overhead lights cast a yellowish glare across the train sheet and train order forms covering his desk. Then one of the lights on the metal box blinked out—that westbound was getting close. Just then the company phone jangled, too. Popeye turned to answer, "Leetone." He was all business.

"Leetonia, this is Wood. I've got BRC-5 at 7:33, number two west, engines 2306, 2244, 2219, 45 loads 22 empties, 5302 tons." It was Homewood Tower, 28.4 track miles to the east, where the mainline climbed from the Ohio River up the Beaver Valley to the top of the grade and made a sharp turn to the west. BRC-5 was a Chicago train, heading to the Belt Railway. And Popeye logged the information across a line on his train sheet, repeating each word and number into the old speaker. Homewood confirmed, and Popeye signed off. BRC-5 would be showing in about fifty minutes. But that first westbound was on the circuit now. We heard his horn, blowing for a crossing on the outskirts of town.

I watched from Popeye's window. In twenty seconds, the crossing lights below started blinking. Bells clanged as the automatic gates began lowering across Walnut Street. A blue Ford pickup scooted across the tracks, hurrying to avoid the wait. The lowered gates halted the next car, and the clanging stopped when the gates came to rest. A few moments of calm at the crossings ... as the approaching rumblings of the train increased. Then the lead diesel appeared from around the bend—beyond the hamburger stand. He was pounding along about 45 on the westbound main, the track closest to the tower, now blowing his warnings for the crossings. The headlight at the center of the engine cut the dusk and swung into the junction as the train rounded the bend. The engineer blew another loud warning, and the town receded into background--train noise filled the junction as the engines roared into the first crossing.

From the high tower I watched him charge toward us, spewing exhaust from engine roof fans. I looked down into the cab and glimpsed the engineer for a second as the lead diesel crossed Walnut and the tower shuddered. Roaring diesels smashed the evening, over the crossing and past. Then the window was filled with the tops of boxcars, flowing from around the bend, a wide river of freight cars, jostling and rocking into the junction and by the

152

tower. And the noise shifted from blaring horns and diesel roar to the beating of steel wheels over switches and rail gaps, the rhythmic four poundings as each car hammered past. And wheel rhythms crashed again-again and again-again and again-again with the thunder of the train. For a long minute, the freight train surged through town, beating its powerful cadence. Then the caboose came into view. It tagged the swaying cars around the bend and rolled closer through the crossings. Popeye waved his electric lantern up and down at the conductor in the cupola as the end of the train passed the tower—all clear—and the last of the train rumbled past and clattered away down the track to the west. Out the opposite tower window, I watched the red marker light on the caboose bob away into the distance, a dutiful, little period chasing after a noisy sentence.

The bells on the crossing gates clanged against fresh stillness as the gates rose up vertical and the flasher lights went out. A couple autos poked out into the calm of the crossings, and Popeye pulled at the company phone and rang up Alliance, the next tower down the line. "CP, this is Leetonia. I've got ED1 by here, 7:41, engines 9648, 9644B, 9785, 7098, westbound track 2, 71 loads, 36 empties, 8104 tons." CP controlled the junction at Alliance, 19.6 miles to the west, where the Cleveland & Pittsburgh line cut across the main to Chicago.

CP confirmed Popeye's information then the operator rattled back at Popeye. "Leetonia, 22 by here at 7:42 pm, engines 5715, 5706, eastbound number 1, 11 cars, 605 tons." Twenty-two was the Manhattan Limited, one of the Pennsylvania's premier passenger trains. He had pulled out of Chicago around noon, heading east. By early tomorrow morning, after an all night run across Pennsylvania and New Jersey, he'd arrive at Penn Station in New York City. He was running on time, which meant he'd pass Leetonia right about 8:02.

Mom and Dad pulled in to the junction a little before eight and parked across the street down below. Dusk was beginning to fall, and it was time to go. I thanked Popeye for letting me hang around, descended the steps behind the tower and walked my bike over to the car. Dad and I loaded the bike into the trunk and tied the trunk down over protruding handlebars. Then we waited a few more minutes to watch 22 come through.

Right on schedule, the final headlight of the day appeared from the west and turned into the straightaway. He came fast, barreling up the mainline, aiming toward the junction. Red flashers clicked on, crossing gates clanged down, and the high-pitched horn of a train again cut the evening air. A glare of headlight grew and grew, then roared into the junction and slammed over the rails. The boom of the train filled crossings and a burst of bright windows followed, heads and shoulders of passengers flashing past in the streaming of long cars. In fifteen seconds he was by, the last car racing away around the sweeping curve to the east, and then gone. Quiet returned. Trackside, relays clicked inside control panels, the crossing gates swung open to clear the street, and the red warning lights blinked dark. As we drove away, I could see Popeye at his desk, framed in the lighted window of the tower... "Wood, I've got 22 at 8:02 pm, engines 5715, 5706...."

On the ride home, a clear night rose up above the hills. Faint stars began to move against the sky, a sliver of moon hung low in the west and the trains of the day settled in. I leaned forward from the backseat toward the soft glow of our dashboard light, and Mom, Dad and I talked about my bright morning ride south, the long afternoon beside the tracks and the muddy creek, and the evening spent within the tower. We talked quietly, as up ahead our headlight beams etched a course homeward.

And somewhere behind, far off across the darkening landscape, beyond the light ebbing from the hills and low valleys of that day, ED1, the Manhattan Limited and the trains of Leetonia journeyed on into the night.

VIII.

Our years compel us to push, to extend, to come to know. So onward we move.   The land offers much--rich forest and hill, lush soft field, easy pathways that beckon forward.   But the terrains may also tease and taunt, with shaded hollows, confused paths and uncertain openings.   There are no signposts for what might lie ahead, no sure promises to guide us.

Cleats

Tough, talented seniors dominated the Canfield Cardinal lineup my junior year.   Gary from the old Pony League Merchants was quarterback, and Ted from the Merchants played fullback.   Gary was fast and could throw a football as well as he threw a baseball. Ted was short, but big-muscled and could run over most anybody. The Cardinal offense was complemented by a solid defense, with Ted anchoring at middle linebacker.   Paul was the hard-nose senior captain—he could take on anyone.   That whole senior squad was just plain good.

From the first day of summer practice, Coach Peterson beat a steady drum for his favorite play--Wing Right 14.   Each practice, every day, the offense drilled that play over and over.   It was basic football--a halfback lined up in wing formation to the right.   At the snap, the halfback and tight end double-teamed the defensive end, the fullback led the play to the right, kicked out on their outside linebacker, and the left halfback took the handoff and followed the fullback into the hole, off the blocks into the secondary.   "Wing Right 14—that's our Bread and Butter Play, men," Coach Peterson reminded us, time and time again.   "You should be able to run it with your eyes closed.   We're going to run it and keep running it-- and make good yards every time."   All season long, over and over, hundreds of repetitions—Wing Right 14, our Bread and Butter Play, the play we Cardinals lived on.

Each player had to learn and practice both an offensive and a defensive position.   On defense, I practiced down guard.   On offense I learned halfback.   I was too small to earn a starting position on varsity offense or defense that year, but the coaches recognized my tackling and effort at practice and I made the kickoff team. Since our offense was good at scoring, most games I had several opportunities to go in on kickoffs. I even got in on some tackles.

One week our starting left defensive guard was injured, and the following Monday at practice Coach Reinhart told me I'd be stepping in to that starting lineman position at our game with Columbiana the end of the week—all 140 pounds of me.

Now, Canfield was a small school—roughly 600 students in grades nine through twelve. We generally played other small, rural schools in and around Mahoning County, so we weren't going up against big Youngstown schools and their rosters of behemoth players. And high school football players back in the 60's weren't nearly as large as players today. But by any measure, 140 pounds for a lineman was puny even then.

That week we practiced and prepared for Friday night's game with Columbiana. From our scouting reports we knew Columbiana's favorite play was the Wedge. The Wedge was their Wing Right 14—their Bread and Butter Play. They'd line up with fullback and two halfbacks in T formation, the quarterback would take the snap, and he'd hand off to the fullback. Their center would shoot straight ahead, the two guards would block down toward the center, their two tackles would block down on the guards, and their two ends would block down on the tackles, forming a human wedge right up the heart of the defense. Then the fullback, led by two blocking halfbacks, would charge straight forward behind the advancing wedge. As a defensive guard, I would have a bird's eye view of all this taking shape and coming at me. The Wedge … their Bread and Butter … I knew it would be coming that game, again and again.

So that week I worked hard on my primary assignment—on the snap, shoot out low and fast, fill the gap between center and their guard, and disrupt the formation of the Wedge. The plan made sense, and I knew I could do it. At the Friday afternoon pep rally in the auditorium I was proud to be introduced with the rest of Canfield's starting defense. No matter that I recently learned the Columbiana lineman who'd be across from me was over 180 pounds and their center was even bigger than that. I knew my assignment. I'd just try harder than them.

156

After the pep rally I was talking with Greg. He didn't play football—basketball was his sport. "So, you're going to start on defense, huh," he said.

"Yeah," I answered.

"How big is their guard going to be?" he asked.

I told him. Greg just looked at me and didn't say anything more.

Today, I have one image of that game, an image gouged into in my mind, play after play. I've just shot out low and fast on the snap, I'm lying stomach down flat on the ground looking out at a sea of football cleats and ankles rushing over me, and I'm trying to peer up through the stampede, catch a glimpse of the football, and then reach out and grab whichever ankle looks to be attached to the ball. That's what I remember. That's it—my worm's eye view of the onrushing tide of steel-tipped cleats and thick ankles.

Canfield won that game—no real thanks to me. I did the best I could, but that wasn't very good. I didn't have a single tackle. After the game, on the team bus ride back home to Canfield, the pride I had felt at the pep rally that afternoon was all but gone—kicked aside and stomped sore under a beating of cleat marks.

At practice the following Monday the team gathered on benches near the locker room for our weekly film review of the prior game. The coaches had studied the Columbiana film over the weekend, so they knew what was coming--the blown plays, missed tackles and solid hits they wanted to critique or compliment. I wasn't looking forward to watching my performance or hearing the coaches' assessment of my play. So somewhere into our viewing of the second half of the game, I was surprised to hear Coach Peterson say, "Now, I want you all to watch Gentzel on this next play."

I couldn't imagine what the film had shown him, since I knew I hadn't made any good plays that night. The 8 millimeter projector sputtered along, as the team watched Columbiana's offense come to the line of scrimmage and get set for the snap. "Now watch. He shoots out low and hard—just like we want," the Coach said as Columbiana snapped the ball. The next second I watched Columbiana's guard trip over me and fall. Then their tackle stumbled into their fallen guard and landed on both of us, and then their end tripped on their tackle and fell into the pile--like a row of dominos! Their ball carrier got hung up in the mess, and a couple of our guys took him down for no gain. "Gentzel took out half their line on that play," the Coach said. "I gave him an assist on that one."

A couple of the seniors spoke up. "Good job, Gentzel." I think they meant it.

Throughout that season, we learned the meaning of a number of old sports sayings from the Coach—"Bread and Butter Play," "Just suck it up" and "It'll be Katy bar the door." I think the Coach liked the "Katy" saying best—he seemed to save it for really special emphasis when a runner broke free and there was no stopping him. But not once did I ever hear the Coach utter another familiar sports saying--"Sometimes it's better to be lucky than good."

Coach Peterson knew he couldn't build a winning team around a core of dumb luck—there was no Dumb Luck 14 play in our Cardinal playbook. But I was glad to see that every now and then, even amid a sea of cleats, a little dumb luck might come sailing along.

Next game our first string guard had healed, and I returned to the kickoff team.

Socks

I wore white socks to school. White cotton socks made sense with tennis shoes and cowboy boots in grade school. After that I kept wearing them--the habit continued with hard sole shoes into junior high and then high school. Most everybody wore white socks in the 50's and early 60's, and I never thought anything about it. But by 1963 or '64 styles had shifted—white was out and dark socks were in.

After I outgrew cowboy shirts with gaudy embroidered horses in early grade school, I lost interest in style. Mom sent me to grade school in a clean pair of jeans, a nice button shirt or T shirt, white socks and tennis shoes. With junior high, I traded in jeans for pants and sneakers for leather shoes. Throughout, I looked like most other guys in school—I was satisfied with that.

Over the years I came to dread the forced march with Mom to Penney's or Sears every August to try on clothes for the new school year. I usually needed a few things, to replace shirts and pants that had worn out or become too small. But I had no interest in searching through the racks of clothes. I hated undressing in the little, no-privacy changing rooms, with straight pins stuck everywhere behind a short curtain, and then having to wander out into the store in pants that didn't fit with sales tags sticking out all over, looking up and down the aisles for Mom so she could grab the waistband to check tightness, turn me around to inspect how baggy the pants were on my rear end, and then send me back to the changing room with yet another pair to try on. It wasn't Mom's fault, of course, and I probably should have been pleased to buy new clothes. But I just wanted to get through the dreaded task as soon as possible, find some decent clothes that fit, and go home. Sock color was a non issue in the ordeal—it had always been white, and white was OK with me.

It was 10th grade when Carol and Nancy saw the problem. My sisters were far more conscious of style than I was. They knew what was in and what was out. The three of us were at home talking one day when they suggested maybe I should get some black socks. "What for?" I said. I was defensive. There was nothing wrong with my socks. White was fine. I had been wearing white for years. What difference did it make?

But following our conversation I began noticing what others were wearing to school. Popular junior and senior guys had black socks. Other kids like me didn't.

I resisted for a long time. White became my little personal badge of honor. White socks or not, I thought I was doing OK. I played football, got good grades…. I had plenty of friends. It didn't seem like the color of your socks should make that much difference, that just by changing your socks you could join the ranks of the cool kids.

By 11th grade most everybody else had shifted over—there were only a few white sock holdouts like me left. One day Mom happened to be around a couple of my friends and me when a sock discussion arose. She listened and then explained to everyone, "Bobby wears white socks because his feet sweat so much." I didn't say anything to her afterwards, but I really wished she hadn't said that. There was no denying it any longer--white socks had become a big problem.

My classmate Rosemary started working on me junior year, talking to me about my socks. I told her the color of a person's socks didn't matter.

Rosemary was smart. "OK," she replied. "If the color of your socks isn't that important, why not wear black sometimes?" she reasoned. I argued with her, but I didn't really have a good counter to her question. We'd go back and forth about sock color a few times, and then she'd stop, look at me, shake her head and say, "You're a dud, a complete dud." Then she'd smile. The next day she was back at it again--she kept at it for weeks. And under the force of her persistence, cracks appeared, and little by little my sock wall began to crumble. It was just a matter of time.

When I eventually asked Mom if I could get a couple pairs of black socks, she understood. I didn't shift over all at once—that would have been too much of a sellout. At first I wore black just every now and then, and then worked up to every other day. Then I got a couple more pairs of dark socks, and wore white only once or twice a week. Within a couple months I just wore black. Rosemary was pleased, and she prodded and coached me along through the transition. Other classmates noticed, too. But after the first day or two of teasing me about black, most everybody was polite and didn't say anything more.

I thought it was all pretty silly and shouldn't have made much difference in how I felt. But it did.

English

In grade school it made sense to learn to read and write and spell. There were comic books to read, street signs to learn, writing on cereal boxes to understand—words were everywhere. Carol could read. All the older kids could read. There was never any question that you would learn, too.

The alphabet song "Now I Know My ABC's" was the foundation. Grade school constructed hours of practice upon that foundation, drawing lines and circles to form letters on special writing paper with blue, horizontal lines. The tall letters like b, h and k fit all the way up and down between the two solid lines. Most letters were only half as tall—they fit between the solid line on the bottom and the dotted line in the middle, like c and n. Some hung down below the bottom line, like p and g. A few, like t and the dot on i, were special because they ended halfway between the dotted line and the top line. To help you learn, every classroom had a large picture of each letter, drawn against those solid and dotted horizontal lines, arranged alphabetically along the top of the front blackboard.

Then it got harder. You learned that each letter had a second, big shape—capital letters. Then harder still, as letters turned into imaginary sounds and the letters and sounds joined together to become words. There was no easy alphabet song to get you through that part—you just had to practice and work until you figured out how those letters and sounds matched up with the words you were already saying every day. And about the time it started making sense, your teacher told you that all along your writing had really only just been printing, and now you would have to relearn all the letters, plus capitals, in something called cursive. If anyone had been keeping score, at that point he might have raised his hand and asked the teacher, "How come we have to learn the same letter five different ways?"

Of course, that was only the beginning--much more was in store for us.

By 5th grade, we had confronted consonants and vowels, weekly spelling lists, spelling rules like "I before E except after C," subjects, verbs, prepositions, direct objects, 250-word theme papers and book reports. While much of the original, practical purpose of learning to read had been achieved—I had mastered comic books and cereal boxes long ago--a few aspects of learning English still made sense. One was spelling lists. Spelling lists were boring, but I could see it was important to spell a word the right way, so a reader wouldn't be confused about what you were trying to say. In spelling, mostly I just memorized the letters. But I also relied on the shape of a word to help me on spelling tests. A word like "pull" started out low and ended high, and so it had a different shape than a word like "able," which started in the middle, was high in the center, and then came back to the middle. A word had to look right for it to be spelled right. And I could understand why some grammar rules, like knowing when to use the singular or plural verb form, made sense. You wouldn't want to say "We was at the fair" or your friends would look at you funny.

But by 5th grade this ongoing study of English had become highly questionable. There were dozens of rules governing spelling—like when to double the consonant before adding a suffix, or when to change a Y to I and add ES. But for every rule it seemed there were exceptions—"or when sounded like A as in neighbor and weigh." And sometimes there were exceptions to the exceptions, with the result that English was full of words that sounded the same but were spelled differently--like toe and tow, boat and vote, bough and bow—or sounded different but were spelled the same—like to bow and curtsy, but bow and arrow, or refuse (to say "no"), but refuse (trash).

So, all those spelling rules were of absolutely no use in the annual class spelling bees. When it was your turn, if you didn't already know how to spell the word the teacher gave you, you could just forget it. You took your best guess at the letters, the teacher confirmed you were wrong, and you sat down and waited another couple rounds for Jane Ann or Mary—one of those girls who had an uncanny knack for spelling—to win again, like she did last year.

All of this English study heaped atop more book reports, writing assignments, and weekend hours wasted in English fiction, and it was obvious the subject had gotten out of hand.

Through junior high and then into high school, spelling lists matured into vocabulary lists; reading assignments grew more laborious; written reports, more exacting and grammar study, more complex. As the work intensified, it seemed the study of English had become a goal unto itself—a student studied English this year for no reason other than to prepare oneself to absorb more English heaped on top of it next year. For a six-week stretch of Mrs. Hall's English class, students toted tall stacks of 3 by 5 note cards and bibliography cards bundled in heavy rubber bands, and Kate Turabian's <u>Manual for Term Papers</u> became every English student's Bible. In this insular environment, the only hint that ever crept into English class of a world beyond high school English was the unnerving admonition ... "You'll need to know this in college."

Carol had graduated and in the fall would leave for college in Bowling Green. On visits home, she would confirm that Mrs. Hall's threat was, regrettably, true.

By junior year, English had expanded to include the study of literature, poetry and novels. And I came to suspect there must be something perverse within English teachers. As ordinary people you might meet on the street, they seemed outwardly OK. I couldn't overlook Mr. Wilhide's rescue of Jack that day in 7th grade. Sometimes you could joke with English teachers and have a little fun in class—they seemed genuinely to care about students. But when I asked myself why an adult would choose to spend a lifetime skewering kids on forced readings of Ivanhoe and The Tale of Two Cities, on essays dissecting incomprehensible lines of 17th century poetry or interpreting the symbolism of Madame Defarge's knitting needles, there was no escaping it. At best, an English teacher was a good person gone astray—more probably, there was a mean streak in there somewhere.

In fairness, I appreciated that teachers weren't solely responsible for the trials of literature study. After all, it wasn't Miss Huberty of 11th grade English who had penned those wordy novels. She wasn't the culprit who employed foreshadowing in Chapter One, or the author who droned on forever describing the whiteness of Moby Dick, or the scoundrel who first cast verse into iambic pentameter. In Great Books discussion one summer we read Shakespeare and Plato and Machiavelli. Their writings were hard to understand. Famous authors had apparently been concocting tales in incomprehensible ways since people could write.

After years of trying to decipher great literature, by 11th grade I finally came to understand the key—it was secrets. Great literature was all about secrets, things only the author knew, and you could be sure he wasn't going to just come right out and tell you. He was going to make you suffer. Great novels were secret truths hidden behind a host of literary contrivances intended to obfuscate—to confuse and perplex English students. What else could it be? No one outside English class ever read these books.

"If the author has something to say, why in the heck doesn't he just say it?" I wondered. "Why does he have to go through page after page of making you try to figure it out?" Secrets ... That was the only answer which made any sense.

So maybe those great authors—not high school English teachers-- were truly the ones with a mean streak. Perhaps high school English teachers were only unwitting accomplices to the evil charade—duped and powerless, like the rest of us pitiful characters in the English tragedy.

Maybe so ... But still, I had my suspicions.

The bell rang to begin English. I placed my notebook on the floor beside my desk and took out my English textbook. The break between periods was never enough time, and many students were still chattering. We had been studying short stories that week, through group discussion in class, and I assumed we would continue that discussion. But Miss Huberty had other ideas.

She surveyed her noisy classroom. "Well, class, I'm glad you're feeling animated this afternoon," Miss Huberty began, "because I have a writing exercise for you." The chattering stopped, and everyone groaned. "Put your text books aside and take out a sheet of paper."

English was a never ending struggle. Every day brought another engagement--a constant battle against similes and metaphors, transitive verbs and dependent clauses. By 11th grade, the fight had settled into a prolonged siege--a sort of trench warfare against all the great authors and legions of grammar rules holed up in enemy lines.

Class discussion of short stories offered some respite. In the battle, group discussion was akin to passing calm hours in the trenches with fellow soldiers. Sometimes the discussion topic was agreeable, and the conversation and camaraderie could temporarily mask your sorry condition. And too, group discussion offered shelter. If you hadn't prepared for class, you could lay low, keep your head down, avoid eye contact with the teacher and stay out of the line of fire.

But there was no relief in writing exercises. When you picked up that pencil, you left the safety of your group huddled in the trench. Now the burden fell squarely upon you, alone. Shelter was gone. Writing assignments were the equivalent of an all out charge--going over the top into battle, exposed to the barrage of every spelling rule, grammar requirement and principle of composition the enemy could hurl at you. In writing exercises, there was no place to hide.

"Now, you'll have twenty minutes," Miss Huberty explained. "You may write about anything you want."

Twenty minutes was no problem. But a wide open topic was a new twist. Normally Miss Huberty's assignments were specific-- employ metaphor to describe a scene from nature, or explain how Thoreau's writing typifies nineteenth century Transcendentalism. A random topic of our choosing was out of character for Miss Huberty. Everyone sat there a moment trying to figure her out.

Sally raised her hand. "I don't understand. Do you mean we don't have a topic?"

"That's right," Miss Huberty answered. "You may choose any topic you want."

"Do you mean any topic from the short stories we've been discussing?" Sally asked.

"Well, you can write about one of the stories if you want. But you can choose something entirely different—anything you want," smiled Miss Huberty.

Jack chimed in, "You mean we can write about anything we want to?"

The class was still struggling with the concept.

"Yes," Miss Huberty repeated. "Write about anything."

"Anything?" Jack asked again.

"Anything," she answered.

A little light flashed in the back of my head--a fresh idea. I turned it over a couple times. It might work.

"OK, class. You have twenty minutes. I suggest you begin."

My idea was bright and compelling. But the concept was also risky. I weighed it for a few moments.... "She might like it," I thought, "or she might really hate it." The assignment would be graded, and grades mattered. I wavered for a second, but the idea was strong. It kept pushing, and I knew I had to take the chance. So I began. At the top of the page, I wrote the title:

Anything Anything: Anything Anything Anything

Then on the first line I started ...

Anything anything anything anything anything anything. Anything anything, anything anything anything anything anything.
"Anything anything anything?" anything anything.
"Anything anything!" anything anything.

And down the page I continued ...

Anything anything, anything anything: anything anything; anything anything anything anything. Anything anything anything--anything anything anything--anything anything. "Anything anything anything! Anything anything anything anything!"

I rattled on, paragraph after paragraph, the words flowing with appropriate punctuation and capitalization. I filled the front of the page, then most of the back, finally bringing my thoughts to an inevitable conclusion:

"Anything anything anything anything?" anything anything.
Anything anything anything.

When time was up, I passed my work forward with others, and we opened our textbooks and resumed class discussion of short stories. After class, worry and second thoughts moved in. I considered justifications for my work: I knew Miss Huberty couldn't take exception to my spelling or punctuation; I was certain my capitalization was faultless; there was no way she could quibble with my logic; and while the content might be considered repetitive, it reflected a precise application of both the spirit and the letter of her instructions. How could she argue with that?
But Miss Huberty understood the underlying battle--she was well schooled in the war and its tactics. She would recognize my essay

for exactly what it was--a defiant thrust out of the trenches, straight into the heart of the enemy—a bold jab with those knitting needles --"Take that Mr. Dickens!" Mine was a risky strike—with one deft stroke of her grading pen she could crush me. At length I concluded my fate lay somewhere beyond the trenches. Only the Muses could save me now—they would determine victory or defeat.

In the hall later that afternoon, I passed a friend who had English with Miss Huberty the period following mine. She gave his class the same impromptu essay assignment. He told me that as he was writing, Miss Huberty was grading papers at her desk when suddenly she burst into laughter, long and hard. It was an auspicious omen.

After the last bell of the day, I headed for my locker to swap books and grab my jacket to board the bus. I closed the locker door and began toward the stairway when I saw Miss Huberty approaching from down the crowded hallway. A few feet away she noticed me, and her mouth curved to a sly smile. "Hello, Bob. Anything new?" she asked as she passed.

Election

The door opened and an assistant from the principal's office walked in to Government class. She went to the teacher and said something quietly. The teacher nodded and turned to the class.

"Jack, you're wanted at the principal's office." Jack looked up. An invitation to the principal's office was not good news.

From the side of the room came a big laugh from Jerry. "Oh HO!" Jerry beamed across at Jack. "The principal's office, eh?"

"Bob, you're wanted, too," the teacher announced.

Now Jerry laughed even louder. We were all friends, and a summons to the office for Jack and me was better yet. "What did you two do?!" Jerry laughed.

"Jerry," the teacher continued, "you're wanted at the office, too." Jerry stopped laughing.

The three of us followed the assistant down the hall. Jack and I had been good friends since 4th grade. Jerry was new to Canfield that junior year—his dad was the new Methodist minister in town. Jerry played football, and we'd become friends. I didn't know why the three of us were being summoned. But I hadn't done anything wrong that I knew of, so whatever it was couldn't be too bad. We walked down the hall, past the site of Mrs. Sturmire's memorable Quadruple Bonk of times past, and turned into the office. The head secretary looked up and motioned to us, "The principal's expecting you. Go on in."

Inside, Mr. Francis asked the three of us to sit down and then smiled. "Congratulations. You've been selected to run for Student Council President." That was big news. Next fall we'd be seniors. Student Council President ran student government for the entire high school.

The Principal discussed the election process. Each of us would have five minutes to address the high school in an assembly early next week. Candidates could place posters and election materials in the halls. The election would be in two weeks. Jack and I had seen elections before, so we understood how it worked. The group talked for a few minutes, and then Mr. Francis wished us good luck. He shook our hands as each of us exited his office.

Later I thought about being selected. I knew each of us wanted the honor, and I was a little uncomfortable with the notion of running against friends. But after a while I figured I'd just do my best, and whatever happened, happened--the competition shouldn't be a problem. I wasn't bothered that the three of us were hand chosen by the administration, or that only guys were selected. It didn't occur to me that there might be others who deserved a chance.

So the Election of '66 was on. Over the next couple days little groups began to coalesce around the candidates, as a few kids migrated toward Jack, Jerry or me. Those individuals became trusted political advisors. I could count on Rosemary and two or three others--maybe my sister Nancy. Ad hoc campaign meetings popped up during lunch and in the halls between classes. Election strategies were mapped out. Mine was a no frills, three-tiered strategy: come up with a slogan, figure out who was going to do the posters, and decide on the best place in the hallway to tape them up. Jack's and Jerry's campaigns were likewise in full swing.

The contest drew out each candidate's personality. I decided to run on sincerity—if elected, I'd do my honest best to represent the students. Jimmy Carter was an unknown then, but he could have modeled his later campaign after mine. Jack was popular, he played guitar in a band—a young Elvis when Elvis was still wholesome. Kids liked Jack. Jerry reminded me of Teddy Roosevelt, a beefy, hard charging guy. In contrast to my simple appeal at the assembly the following week, Jerry's speech was full of solid campaign promises and concrete actions he would take if elected—I was impressed.

Then something unexpected happened. It's not clear where it came from or how it started. It just seemed to spring up, a grass roots movement--Fred for Student Council President!

Fred was my neighbor, a couple years younger. His family had moved to Canfield from Youngstown some years earlier. When I was in grade school and junior high, Fred and I were friends. He did a lot of construction work on the tree house in the willow. Together we built a sod dam with spillways across the creek in his back yard, shot BB guns, and one winter built a snow fort ten feet tall. Summers we fished for sunfish and bullhead catfish in the creek. But as we grew older our paths diverged. Fred wasn't interested in sports, and he didn't care about school or report cards. He got a pellet gun that could take down birds, and he enjoyed trapping muskrats in the creek and skinning them. Skinning wasn't for me.

After a visit to Fred's basement one day, where I watched him prying open bullets in a vice to collect gunpowder, we quietly parted company. There was no malice or animosity—we just went our separate ways. Later Fred began hanging around some of his old Youngstown friends—city kids were a tougher breed than us country kids. So by my junior year Fred and I weren't really friends anymore. But some respect remained between us, a mutual acceptance of the other in his separate turf.

On the bus, I heard kids talking about a write in campaign for Fred. Soon election posters for Fred began appearing next to hall lockers. I think Fred got a kick out of it, and he teased the movement along—half fun, half serious. The movement to elect Fred took hold and became a big part of the election.

But Fred and everyone else knew he wasn't the kind of student Mr. Francis would ever select to run for Student Council President. Fred wasn't part of the approved ruling class, like Jerry, Jack and me. Fred had elected a different path, his own way of doing things.

169

He approached school differently. So everyone knew the school administration would throw out votes for Fred. But that was exactly the point--a vote for Fred was a protest vote against the system, against a rigged election.

Fred and I talked some on the bus and kidded each other about the election during those couple of weeks. I wanted to win, but I thought it was OK that Fred had a cheering section.

The day the winner was announced, Jerry, Jack and I were again seated on stage in front of the school. Fred was somewhere in the audience, up in the bleachers with the rest of the freshmen. When Mr. Francis announced that Jack had won, a lot of juniors in the front of the audience leapt to their feet, clapping. I congratulated Jack and shook his hand--I was disappointed, but happy for Jack.

Jack went to the podium center stage and delivered his acceptance speech. Jerry and I sat off to the side. We were the losers. Yet being on stage in front of the school was an affirmation of sorts. Jerry and I were afforded an opportunity to be gracious losers--that's a big difference. A loser ignored is just a loser; a gracious loser can salvage a little dignity.

It didn't occur to me at the time—for the school would never have permitted it--but it might have been a nice gesture to have allowed Fred to be seated on stage with Jerry and me that day, affording him the same respect. After all ... who knows? Fred might actually have won.

Prom

The prom flushed you out of hiding. Years of ignoring girls, of keeping a safe distance, of hanging back came to an end with the prom. The prom forced you into the open, to step forward into the world of girls and dates.

It had been coming on for a while. Through freshman and sophomore years, the signs were there. The days of group teasing over boyfriends and girlfriends had ceased in junior high. Interest in the opposite sex had blossomed, and even a few 9th and 10th grade boys and girls were beginning to go together. The notion of couples began to take hold. Couples were common among upperclassmen at school. When a couple passed in the hallways, you didn't stare, but you viewed couples with silent envy. Couples made you feel lacking, juvenile. Going with someone, going steady, was a major advance beyond what grownups called adolescence. It wasn't clear how we underclassmen would get there. There wasn't a set progression, like from Latin I to Latin II to Latin III, where you just enrolled and then followed the rules. It seemed more haphazard, a matter of fits and starts, of chance--like the Irish Sweepstakes. Despite the odds, we underclassmen somehow silently believed our couple time was coming, too ... eventually.

Through sophomore year and junior year, girls focused on prom preparation work, of drawing guys out into the open. Girls did the initiating. A common technique was the Saturday night party. One of your classmates would talk her parents into letting her invite about a dozen kids to her home. The event was carefully staged. She and her girlfriends would select the boys to be asked, with an eye toward preferred pairings. You knew it was a set up. But your friends would be there, it wouldn't be polite to refuse, and the group expected you to attend. There'd be potato chips and pop, and you were kind of interested in going. Her parents were always in the next room.

Hanging out at the party, talking, eating pretzels and joking around was OK. Knowing that you were unofficially paired up with someone wasn't necessarily bad—the party cast you in the role of being on a date, but in an easier group setting. It was the records and dancing that felt awkward, contrived. Always there was dancing. For some reason girls just liked to dance—for them it was fun. For me it was a forced exercise. I tried, went through the steps and the movements, but I just felt silly making my body flail around in somebody's nonsensical, socially prescribed ways. Fortunately, girls could see dancing was a struggle for a lot of guys, and so at parties they tried to help us learn the motions and not feel too awkward. They seemed to have your best interests in mind.

Preparing for the big dance was a major production. Each year the junior class was responsible for planning, decorating and conducting the Junior/Senior Prom. Work began weeks in advance, and by the time the dance arrived almost every junior became involved. There were planning sessions with class officers and teacher advisors, refreshment and decorating committees, groups set up to select a band and individuals designated to buy cardboard, paint, masking tape and crepe paper.

The central task was decorating the gym, transforming that arena normally reserved for jumping jacks and dodge ball into a Saturday night ballroom. And so Sally, Lela and the group of creative girls who could draw, the ones with imagination enough to envision elegance rising up from gym bleachers, basketball hoops and stark, wooden floors, took charge of theme and decorating scheme. And the more practical kids, the guys, the class officers, the ones who usually ran things, stepped back and took their lead from the artful girls.

Weeks of planning culminated with prom week. Monday morning the school locked the gym doors and turned over the keys to the junior class. Juniors were excused from study halls that week to decorate—a new shift of decorators each period. There were cardboard sheets to paint with big black and white squares simulating floor tiles and walkways, tall green ferns and plants to construct, guy wires to run back and forth across the gym, stately white pillars and twinkling chandeliers to build, pastoral murals to paint, velvet curtains to hang and sound system wiring to conceal. Work continued beyond the school day and into the evenings.

Crepe paper tied it all together—rolls and rolls of pastel crepe paper twisted and draped throughout. We filled each nook and corner of the old gym with the paper ribbons. With tall ladders borrowed from the janitors, we hung crepe paper walls, masked the bleachers, and flowed the strands back and forth across the ceiling, always with the uniform number of twists between guy wires. And as the weekend approached, thousands of strands of crepe paper came to envelop a fanciful little world.

Earlier that school year, in the same gym and auditorium, Jane Ann, Dave, Paul, Lela, Nancy, Paula and a small group of other juniors had staged the Junior Class play. "Dirty Work at the Crossroads" was a spoof of an 1890's melodrama with villain, innocent heroine and stout-hearted hero. "They're really good," I thought as I sat in the audience and watched them perform. This was our class play, but only a fraction of the class was involved.

The prom drew in almost all juniors—the kids who never stood center stage, average students who received scant recognition, kids who each day quietly went about their business. Together, popular kids and classmates more accustomed to the background left study hall, merged in the gym each period and set themselves to twisting rolls of crepe paper, bringing parallel strands into conformance. Somebody brought in a transistor radio, and the shifts twisted along to the music of Peter, Paul and Mary, to the Mama's and Papa's "Monday Monday."   Most school activities sliced and sorted students into a hierarchy of individual grades, rankings and classifications. This was different. Prom week was a time of parallel tasks--always the same number of twists, an exercise in conformance. Prom week conferred Class.

And each time a new shift of decorators opened the gym door and a fresh breeze blew in, our curtain of crepe paper strands billowed and waved as one.

Musical chairs was a popular game at grade school birthday parties. As the music played, Kathy and Beverly, Jimmy and Larry and all the other kids would circle the chairs slowly, each player positioning to jump and claim a seat—don't be the odd person left standing when the music stopped. Finding a date for the prom was the high school version of musical chairs.

By mid April our class had begun the slow circling. Boys and girls moved in a calculated silence, weighing the chances of claiming a date--someone you actually wanted to go with—and not being odd man out when the dance music started. Couples were lucky--they didn't have to worry about whom to ask. But the rest of us had to confront the issue. Guys did the asking, so pressure was on the Mike's and Tim's and Larry's and Richy's to be decisive, step forward and ask, and not wait until the last minute. For all the Doreen's and Lemoine's and Jane's and Chris', early May was an anxious time of waiting for the right guy to appear, and worrying what to say if the wrong guy approached. We all moved together in the calculated circling. But for each, it was a solitary maneuver.

Since Valentine's Day in grade school, matters of the heart had remained confusing. Back then I didn't know which girls should receive a Valentine and which ones I should ignore. I didn't want to hurt anyone's feelings, but I didn't want to give a card to just any girl. In second grade, there was no clear way to decide. By 11th grade, I was still lost. But now it was prom time, and the question had to be answered: should I ask Rosemary or Elizabeth?

Rosemary was the logical choice. We weren't a couple, but we had become friends over the last year. I liked her. Rosemary had coached me through my conversion to black socks, sometimes we were paired at Saturday night parties, and she did her best to help me learn to dance. She had effort invested in me. Rosemary was smart, well-liked, fun to be with, and I thought she probably wanted me to ask.

There was no logical reason to ask Elizabeth. I had first noticed her back in grade school—she was tall and pretty. Over the years we never interacted much. She was good in art, but I couldn't draw. She became popular in junior high, and I envied the guys who were forward enough to tease her about the clumsy way she played basketball. But I didn't play basketball. I liked talking with her whenever the chance arose, but always she seemed to be passing by, moving in other directions. So conversations were infrequent. But the trouble was, I was attracted to her.

I didn't want to hurt Rosemary's feelings. By high school, all the teachings and admonitions over the years to be kind and considerate to others had long since sunk in. I understood it was wrong to do something hurtful to another. It wasn't just teachings and Sunday school rules that came to bear—I didn't want to hurt Rosemary because I cared about her.

But as the concept of couples emerged in high school, another rule seemed to rise up and take hold. It wasn't a rule taught in Sunday school or part of a Boy Scout oath. It wasn't voiced in a simple adage, like the Golden Rule. Rather, it was unspoken, hazy-- something grownups didn't talk about. It arose from self interest, squeezed up from somewhere under the pressure of prom time. I wasn't consciously mindful of the notion, but it found me and sought to assert itself. Put into words, the rule would have read something like "Do unto others as you would have others do unto you--unless there's a pretty girl involved."

Mom didn't have this "Pretty Girl Exception" in mind when she encouraged me to give Valentines to everyone in second grade. But that was different. By high school, I had come to realize that men might apply this "Pretty Girl Exception" to lots of rules—like "Thou shall not lie--unless there's a pretty girl involved." In church you learned that people who strictly followed the base rule—the "Thou shall not" part of the rule--without applying the Exception, had character. Outside church, you learned that those who took advantage of the Exception had fun. I wanted to believe I had some character—but fun didn't seem like such bad an idea, either.

To make matters worse, another confusing notion compounded my dilemma—an idea that seemed to justify the "Pretty Girl Exception." Being selfish was, of course, a bad thing. But in matters of the heart, I began to sense that it might be OK to be selfish. As with the Exception, people didn't come right out and state the notion. But grownups I respected seemed to endorse the thought that it was OK to recognize your feelings and follow where they led—even if it meant someone else's feelings could be hurt. It was a sad fact of life that even caring moms couldn't change.

So I decided to ask Elizabeth.

It took a couple days to figure out the least awkward way to do it. My plan was to ask when Elizabeth was at her hall locker at the end of the school day. I knew she would be there, since everyone went to the lockers after the final bell to sort through books and notebooks before hurrying downstairs to the catch the buses. I didn't know that she would say "Yes," but I thought we had been friends enough over the years that she might agree. If she said "No," it was going to be embarrassing. So I wanted a time and place when people were busy and wouldn't notice our conversation, and where I'd have a reason to leave quickly, if necessary.

When the final bell rang, I made a bee line to my locker and picked up a couple books to carry home. Then I hurried through the crowded halls to where Elizabeth would be. There she was, standing alone in front of her open locker door, pushing some books inside. I took a deep breath and walked over to her. When I was a few feet away, she happened to look up and notice me.

"Hi, Elizabeth," I said.

"Oh, hi, Bob," she replied. Her face had vacant stare.

Second thoughts hit, but I had come too far. "I was wondering if you'd like to go to the prom with me."

She listened as I spoke, and she hesitated a second. Then in a cool, matter-of-fact tone Elizabeth faced me and announced "That would be against my better judgment."

"Huh?" I thought. "… against her better judgment?" I was expecting an answer like "Yes" or "No" or "I already have a date." Her reply threw me off—it sounded like a rehearsed line in a play. It took a couple seconds for her statement to register before I concluded she was telling me "No."

"Oh. Well then … ah … OK," I stumbled. I was embarrassed, and she seemed a little embarrassed, too. "Well, thanks anyway," I said and turned and walked away.

If I had been cool and had my wits about me, instead of just walking away, I might have joked and quipped something like, "I see … against your better judgment, eh? Well, what might your not-so-good judgment have to say about it? What do you think, Elizabeth? Is that something we might be able to work with?" Some words like that might have broken the ice and allowed each of us to feel less awkward.

But at that moment I was a long, long way from being cool. I was just flustered and glad I had a reason to leave in a hurry—at least that part of my plan worked out.

A few days later I asked Rosemary. I didn't feel quite right about asking her—she deserved better. But I was pleased when she said "Yes." She had been patiently waiting on me, just like she had with my white socks.

Elizabeth went to the prom with a senior—I guess she had been waiting for him to ask when I bumbled along.

In the end, all my awkward wrestling with jumbled notions of right and wrong and conflicting feelings over which girl to ask didn't much matter. Instead, that calculated slow circling, the old force of that turning of boys' way against girls' way, came to bear and churned forth one more prom pairing.

The night of the prom Rosemary looked really pretty, and we had a special time dancing under tin foil chandeliers and a sky of crepe paper.

IX

Clouds amass, towering white, billowing, majestic from afar. It builds ... and within, an expanse of darkness approaches. Breezes gust and the wind turns ragged. The rumbling comes low and threatening, ominous, approaching.

It hits with force and shakes the forests, explodes upon soft living things clinging to the surface. Fury and thunder shudder deep into the rocks, and long echoes tremble the lands, surging into valleys and rolling over hillsides. It storms down against the earth, forging and tearing, gashing and gushing at earthen forms, at its nature. Earth and soil are cut, and roots of soft living things strain to hold fast in their place.

Passing

During summers I worked with Dad. He installed and repaired Carrier air conditioning units at factories, offices and homes throughout Mahoning and Columbiana counties. He handled all the technical work—where you had to understand how refrigeration systems functioned--and I helped with simple, physical work, like putting up ductwork in cramped spaces, washing electronic air cleaners, carrying tools, and helping run copper lines to rooftop condensing coils. Summer was the busy season, with daily calls from new customers wanting relief from the heat and existing customers who needed their systems serviced or repaired. Each morning Dad and I ate an early breakfast then headed out in his Ford Econoline van for a day of hard work. By about 5:30 we'd find a break point in the job, load tool boxes of Crescent wrenches, channel locks and tin snips back into the Ford, and drive home to Pleasant Valley Lane for supper.

We'd been working in East Palestine, putting in a new cooling system at the Nash offices, a tool and die factory on East Taggart Street. Up and down stairs and ladders, in and out of the van all day fetching tools, crawling through cubby holes, lugging ductwork and welding equipment, the work was hot and sweaty. But late afternoon a fierce thunderstorm hit, gusting into town from the northwest and pushing through with a burst of hard rain. When we gathered up toolboxes, drills and extension cords at the end of the day and climbed into the van to head home, a hint of ozone from the storm still lingered.

Up county road 165, through North Lima, across Western Reserve, and along Tippecanoe Road, the van splashed through leftover puddles from the afternoon rain. As we neared home, I was looking forward to taking a shower, having dinner, then a long workout session with my weights. Down Pleasant Valley, and as Dad slowed to turn into the driveway, I glanced across the side yard toward the pond. And my eyes told me something was wrong—the picture was off. I felt it before I could think it—the form of the big willow and my tree house was missing! My head flashed "No" trying to deny my eyes. I refocused. The big willow was toppled over, my tree house smashed on its side against the ground. The storm had taken them down. Where the big tree stood that morning was now a void against the evening sky.

Dad parked the van by the garage, and we got out. Mom came outside to meet us, explaining about the storm. Quietly we walked around the pond to the fallen tree. It was a confusion of thick wood, broken boughs and branches and willow leaves sprawled across the yard. Within the jumble of treetop, some of the tree house was still intact—those big two-by-six's across the roof didn't give up easy. But walls and floor were splintered, and the base of the big willow trunk was broken apart, all twisted and torn.

I hadn't spent much time in the tree house since junior high. I had outgrown BB guns and playing with boats in the pond. But I hadn't outgrown knowing what that big tree and its home of hand-me-down boards once meant. I kicked through the branches, wanting somehow to raise the whole tree back upright, to restore its standing and fill the void. But I knew gravity had won.

It took a couple weeks for the saws and chainsaws methodically to reduce the willow. The wood was carted off. I tore apart tree house boards, smashed at the broken lumber with hammer and crowbar, and made a big pile of the remains near where it had crashed down. And when the tearing was done, one evening at dusk I took a match and lit the pile.

At its height, the bonfire whipped ten feet upward and sent plumes of sparks scattering into the night sky. Dad and I stood back and watched, and the sharp light from the fire crackled and beat

179

against the darkness. After a while, as the flames and sparks tempered lower, I tended the edge of the fire, tossing ends of boards not yet consumed back into the center flames. It took a couple hours for the fire to take the boards, till all that was left was a big bed of ash, bent nails and smoky coals glowing up from the ground. Dad went back inside. I kept watch a while longer, till the heat died out, darkness spread its hold, and the warmth of the fire was gone.

I always knew that willow couldn't last forever. But that didn't stop my wishing it would.

Fair

"It's not FAIR!" shouted Nancy. Tears welled up in her eyes, and her little face was red with anger. Carol had taken Nancy's sailor hat and wouldn't give it back. In the front yard at Palmyra Road, Nancy was three and Carol six. Nancy jumped and strained to grab the hat away, but Carol held it high overhead, well above Nancy's reach. Carol was just too big. Nancy planted herself in front of Carol, tears running down her cheeks, and with all the force her little lungs could muster, screamed again in Carol's face, "It's NOT FAIR!"

At three years old, Nancy hadn't been educated in the concept of justice. But she didn't need teaching—something inside already knew what was fair and what wasn't.

The Canfield Fair was second only to the Ohio State Fair in Columbus. Thursday before Labor Day, thousands from northeast Ohio began streaming to the fairgrounds on the south edge of Canfield. By the end of the long Labor Day weekend, over a hundred thousand would be drawn through the gates to ride the Ferris wheel and Tilt-a-Whirl, stroll crowded midways, enjoy Italian sausage sandwiches and salted vinegar French fries, watch calf judging and draft horse pulls, ogle shelves of blue ribbon apple pies

180

and raspberry preserves in the 4-H building, and to test their luck winning teddy bears and carnival kewpie dolls at shooting galleries and ring toss booths—"Four shots for a quarter!" the pitchmen sang out. Attractions filled the fairgrounds, stocks of Mother Nature's bounties--all the best life had to offer was there for the sampling. For those of us counting the dwindling days of summer vacation, the Canfield Fair was the last great hurrah of summertime before another year of school began.

But the Fair collided head-on with two-a-day summer football practice. After two weeks of double practices, if you had any energy left you could visit the Fair on Sunday—our lone day off. But every other day, even Labor Day, football ruled absolutely. Like Coach Peterson before him, Coach Phillips accepted no excuse for missing football practice. We were a team, and every player knew he was expected to contribute his all.

Rick lived on his family's farm south of town. He had never struck me as interested in sports, so I was surprised when he went out for football senior year. Rick was quiet, likeable, bigger than average. Through his responsibilities over the years on the farm, I imagine he had learned the meaning of work. And now he wanted to become a lineman on the football team.

At practice midweek, just before the Fair opened, the team became aware of Rick's problem. As a 4-H project, Rick had raised a calf that year and entered it in competition at the Fair. The judging would be Friday during football practice, and Rick had to be present at the judging for his calf to qualify.

Rick and Coach Phillips worked out a deal—I suspect Rick's parents may have become involved. At the end of Thursday practice, with the team resting on one knee with helmets off, the Coach delivered his daily wrap up, pointing out our progress and stressing the hard work which remained. He was still learning about each of the players on his new team, feeling his way along. Then the Coach informed us, "Now ... Rick's not going to be at practice tomorrow—he's chosen calf judging instead." Guys glanced over at Rick, but he just listened like the rest of us, keeping his eyes focused straight ahead. The Coach continued, "Rick's going to miss all the fun the rest of us will be having out here practicing while he's off at the Fair." Rick held his firm expression. "So when Rick's back at

181

practice Saturday, we're going to have a special drill … just for him."
Rick understood full well what that meant—it was going to hurt.
But you could see in that hard focus of his eyes, Rick was prepared
to accept it. That calf must have meant a lot to him.

Friday practice proceeded normally, without Rick, and Saturday
morning he was back in the locker room, suiting up with the rest of
us.   Saturday was another hot day.   Between the counts and
cadences of our football drills, shouts of Coach LeVan at missed
assignments and dropped balls, and the thud of tired bodies
colliding through the afternoon, noise from the Fairgrounds a half
mile across town drifted over the practice field. Faint hurdy-gurdy
music of the Ferris wheel mixed with the hum of the midway and
the distant PA system announcing lost children and misplaced fair
goers.   "Mr. Kenner, Mr. Kenner, please meet your family at the
Poultry Barn, that's the Poultry Barn." More hum from the midway
… then "We have a lost boy here at the booth. He says he's four
and name is Johnny. He wants to go home. Would Johnny's
parents please come to the Information Booth at the big rock by the
grandstands to claim him."   Then more thuds of helmets hitting
against shoulder pads and mean shouts as tacklers wrestled
teammates to the ground.

Coach Phillips saved Rick's time for the end. It was one of our
usual defensive drills. The team formed a circle with Rick in the
middle. "Jackson" the Coach called. And Jackson broke from the
circle and ran at Rick, trying to flatten him with a block, as you'd do
playing offense. Rick's job was to meet the blocker, fend him off
and remain standing.   Jackson hit Rick and knocked him back a
couple steps. Jackson returned to the circle, and the Coach called
another name. "Ok … Barton—go get him." And Barton ran full tilt
at Rick and knocked him sideways. But Rick met him and kept his
feet. The Coach called another name, and then another, and each
time Rick battled to defend himself.

Normally the same guy remained in the middle for six or eight
hits. Then the Coach would relieve the defender to return to the
circle, and order someone else to enter the middle. But this wasn't
a normal drill—there were no relief plans in this one. "You can't
improve your football skills at the Fair," the Coach reminded

everyone. Rick panted hard, trying to catch his breath. "Simpson, go block that man!" the Coach called out.

Rick managed to hold his own through the first eight or ten guys. But the punishment was taking a toll. The Coach shouted another name, "Jenkins." And Jenkins came hard at Rick and knocked him to the ground. Rick pulled himself up and turned to face the next. The Coach called another name, and the next blocker again knocked Rick down. After Rick regained his feet, another player came hard and knocked him into the dirt again—Rick didn't have much left. But each time Rick managed to raise himself up and stand to face the next man—and the Coach called another name, then another. Rick about had it.

The Coach yelled, "Webster!" Webster broke from the circle and knocked Rick from the side, and Rick fell to the ground against his arm. He grabbed at his forearm and twisted off the ground back up to his knees. Then he managed to stand—barely--cradling his arm. Some guys might fake being hurt to put an end to it. I didn't know if Rick was faking—he might have been. But then he didn't seem like the kind of kid who'd do that. "Gentzel!" the Coach yelled. Rick turned my direction, and I ran at him and leveled a hard block chest high, just like I always did in the drill. I knocked him back, and he cringed with his arm to his side. I returned to the circle. The Coach called another name, Rick did his best to protect himself, then at last the Coach stopped. It was over. Rick struggled to get up. Practice was done, and the Coach dismissed the team.

As we turned and jogged away from the field, Coach LeVan went to Rick and eased his helmet off, trying to help. Rick knelt on one knee, cradling his arm. He grimaced—the firm calm in Rick's eyes from two days before was gone.

People usually try to do the right thing. Rick was trying to be a responsible 4-H'er. Coach Phillips was trying to be fair, allowing Rick to miss practice so he could complete his 4-H project. But the Coach had a responsibility to the rest of the team, too, to those of us who didn't get the day off. So Rick needed to pay a price for the privilege of missing practice and breaking team rules. Fairness needed to hurt. Rick understood the drill.

But even when people try, sometimes the right thing doesn't work out. Something unexpected, unforeseen snaps, and before we know what's happened, those good intentions don't matter anymore. The limit between what's OK and what's "over the line" isn't always clear—you might not realize you've passed the line until you find yourself there. Nobody—not the Coach, not Rick or anyone else out there on that field--nobody wanted it to end like that.

When I arrived home from practice that day, I didn't mention anything about Rick and the drill. But it didn't take long for the phone to ring and Mom to hear the story. She hung up and quickly confronted me in the hallway. "Did you knock Rick down, too?" She was upset and wanted to know. I nodded and lowered my eyes. "Bobby ... How could you?!" Mom was shocked. She couldn't believe her son would do such a thing. "That's communism!" she shouted at me.

In Government classes at school, we had studied communes, the Soviet Union, the system of laboring for the state and the common good. So I knew, strictly speaking, communism was actually a form of government, and Mom was wrong. But I didn't say anything more. I knew what happened at practice that day shouldn't have happened. I knew what I did was wrong. Fair had turned unfair. And Mom wasn't all that far off.

Pageant

Canfield was growing, and a new high school opened senior year. We left the old school on Wadsworth Street, and grades nine through twelve were uprooted to the new C. M. Johnson building off Route 224, just east of the Erie crossing.

The move created changes for the football team. There was no field at the new school, so practice shifted to the old Pony League baseball field off Lisbon Street. After school, the team suited up in the locker room and then jogged a half mile up to the ball field. Leaving the school yard, we cut across to the Erie tracks, then followed the railroad south over 224 to a short dirt road leading to the ball field. Jogging along the tracks in steel cleats--over uneven ties on loose ballast--was a herky-jerky exercise in keeping your feet from getting caught and ankles twisted in the gaps between ties. Our daily trek along the tracks was a mismatch—football didn't belong out on a railroad, stumbling along toward a baseball field. Clomping along the tracks in mud-stained practice jerseys, the Cardinals must have looked like some vagabond team searching for a home. It felt demeaning.

Saturday afternoon home games produced another change. In this case our move to the new school produced a more noble result.

Varsity games continued on the field behind the old high school. On Saturday game days, the team met at the new school and suited up. Then a couple of school buses shuttled the team to the old school, stopping on Wadsworth in front of the building, positioning the team for our entrance. We stepped off the buses, slipped on our helmets, and readied for our stately jog up the asphalt bus circle, past the old memorial school bell, past the tall steel doors of the main high school entrance off to the right, under the tight second story brick overpass connecting elementary school to old high school, and opening to the backside of the school yard. As we stepped from the buses, we could hear the growing pregame hubbub from the field behind the school. Marching bands were warming up, snare drums rattled, trumpets were calling and cheering sections were mustering up strength. The noise spilled out from the bleachers and carried over the village.

Game day uniform was calculated—polished black shoes, clean white socks, black pants with sheen, and white jerseys with bright, bold red block numbers and trim. Black helmets glistened with their battle scars of scuffs and scrapes--on each side an image of a Cardinal head, blood dripping from the beak. Eyes solemn, edged with grease war paint, peered out from behind face masks. As the mass of players began to move, the air filled with muffled flaps of shoulder pads and dangling chin straps, and the sharp clatter of steel-tipped cleats on pavement. We jogged slowly, intent--silent but for the clatter. Students, parents and community walking across the school grounds toward the game now stopped and stepped aside, respectfully, to let the football body pass. Our pace picked up, and the clatter grew stronger. Small children watched from their parent's side as the team surged past. Then faster, the

185

racket hardened into ringing echoes as we entered the overpass. Emerging with a shout, our procession burst forth from the opening and rushed forward onto the field. Stand aside! We were the Canfield Cardinals, and we were ready for the fight.

The pageantry of that moment never hit me till years later. Jogging toward the field, I was mindful only of the contest about to unfold, immersed in my football X's and O's, focused on executing my assignments and the demands of the game. The notion of pageantry was foreign--the only pageant I knew was the annual Miss America contest on TV, and that had nothing to do with me.

But that Saturday entrance ritual was a pageant, with the same elements that must have infused similar scenes centuries before ... when knights in armor rode out from their castle to meet an enemy in battle. Within castle walls peasants and townspeople would clear a path to the gate as the column of knights approached; the measured clattering of horse hoofs on cobblestone would merge with the clanking of armor, chain mail, swords and lance as the procession rode past. Young children looked up. Beneath bold colors and banners waving, the young men rallied round a bright coat of arms, carried along by honor and a sacred oath of loyalty to the city-state. The gates would then open, from somewhere a trumpet sounded, and the stern column of warriors would ride out to do battle.

Of course our 20th century battle was far less terrible and lacked the bloody finality of theirs. Their vanquished did not return from the field. We Cardinals were fortunate, as a more merciful order had come to prevail in our arena, graciously permitting the vanquished to rise up and try again next weekend.

Fitch

Each season Canfield varsity played Austintown Fitch. It was the one game in Canfield's schedule where we confronted a team way out of our league. Unlike our usual, small rural opponents, Fitch was a big Youngstown city school. They were a football force, a powerhouse, always going to the playoffs and competing for regional titles. No one expected Canfield to win the annual game with Fitch—for years the game was a predictable, one-sided affair. But that changed freshman year.

186

It was an away game in Austintown. Since freshmen weren't part of the varsity, that Friday night I watched from the stands and cheered with the rest of the crowd. It was a tough game. Fitch was in control the first half, but Canfield fought hard and hung in. The second half remained a close contest. Late in the 4th quarter, Canfield trailed by seven points. With time running short, Canfield mounted a long drive that broke into the end zone for six. And with time running out, the Cardinals went for the win and converted on a gutsy two-point pass. Canfield boosters erupted! A proverbial storybook upset! Fitch hung their heads in stunned silence. David had slain Goliath, and the Canfield faithful celebrated their football miracle into the night. The following day the sports page of the <u>Youngstown Vindicator</u> was aglow with the account of Canfield's improbable victory.

But amid the joy, that great victory for Canfield football created an unforeseen, troubling legacy for future seasons: if the Cardinals could do it once, why not again?

It was late in the season, senior year. Through the fall, the team had shared a few bright spots—Roger was chosen team captain thanks to his solid tackling; George, Jim, Richy and Jerry had proven their toughness on defense; Danny had made some acrobatic catches for big gains; and his brother Terry had run back an interception for a touchdown in our 30 – 14 win over Poland. But our losses outnumbered the wins.

The team had a good week of practice leading up to the Fitch game. We were able to put our mediocre season behind us, and players and coaches brought renewed energy and commitment to those practice sessions. Whooping, hollering and hitting from Monday through Thursday we pushed and cheered ourselves onward, and by Friday afternoon's pregame practice we had convinced ourselves that we actually had a chance. We knew we were a big underdog, but the thought had taken root that maybe, somehow, we could pull it off. Forget our disappointing performance to date--a victory over Fitch would erase all that and redeem the entire season.

The town was behind us—Friday evening the Boosters Club served the team steak dinners at the Skylark restaurant before the game. Then school buses departed the village and conveyed us north on 46 to Austintown for the night game at their stadium—the same field where Canfield had wrestled that storybook finish from Austintown three years before. The evening brought good football weather—clear skies and temperatures down in the 50's. Fitch won the toss and elected to receive. On the kickoff they got a good return across midfield and into Canfield territory. Then our defense came in to confront them on the first play from scrimmage.

I played safety, normally on the right side. I was fair defending against the pass, but played pretty well at coming up and stopping the run for short gains. On that first play Fitch handed off to one of their halfbacks who came shooting around my side. I came up on him, and in a flash he made a cut to the outside. I reacted, stretched out and was barely able to get my hands on him and twist him down for a four yard gain. When I hit him, he was solid. As I got up from the tackle I thought "Geez he's fast! I almost missed him." I hadn't seen any halfbacks move that quick before. I was used to making those kind of tackles routinely, and the thought that he almost got by me was unsettling. A few plays later Fitch rammed the ball into the end zone for their first score.

By the middle of the first quarter the writing was on the wall. Fitch would kick off to Canfield and force a three and out--our offense was no match for them. After receiving the punt, it didn't take Fitch's offense long to march down the field and score again. They came around the right, they came left, they came up the middle—it didn't matter where they came. They just kept coming. That offense was a machine. Each series, they grabbed big chunks of yards every play. They were relentless.

Canfield kept up some energy and enthusiasm through much of the first half beating. But by mid game, the only inspired shouting from the Canfield side was Coach Phillips in the locker room, trying to encourage us at halftime. "Come on! You're better than this! What's going on out there?!" he yelled. We hung our heads. None of us had any answers.

Somewhere in the third quarter, Fitch put in their second string. But it didn't make any difference. I got beat, time and again by their runners and receivers. The hope and commitment of that week were mashed into defeat, till all that was left was bruised anger quivering with a little stubborn pride. I continued throwing myself into every play, clapping, trying to encourage myself and teammates on defense—despite the disaster. But somewhere in the fourth quarter, on one of their runs up the middle, the ball was snapped, and in an instant a stampede of big Fitch linemen smashed through our defensive line, ran over our linebackers and came zeroing in on us safeties. It was a rout, they were upon me, and the thought flashed over me--"Man! I could get hurt out here."

Sixty-two to nothing ... That was the final score. I guess Austintown missed an extra point on one of their touchdowns somewhere along the way, or it would have been 63 to nothing. In school on Monday, Polly and Charlene, two of sister Nancy's friends who had been at the game, were talking with a couple of us on the team. "So, when did you guys just give up?" Charlene asked. I was too ashamed to answer her, but I thought of that play with Fitch linemen charging up field, looking for more victims.

They say you're supposed to be able to draw something positive out of the defeats, some little morsel of hope or renewed conviction, some twist in perspective that comforts or helps sustain you through the disappointment. Something to affirm your worth, lift your spirit and encourage you to hold your head high ...

They're wrong. There ain't nothing positive about 62 to nothing. Absolutely nothing.

X.

With each new light, we are made to rise. We seek the highlands, where the light is strong and the earth underfoot feels solid. Unexpected, our path may turn and open upon a clear vista, a point from which we might see out and remark the way we've come. While far beyond, a high distant horizon still awaits our approach.

The view brings perspective. And so at that spot, that clearing, we may pause and for a time find shade and comfort, healing and ease. A high bluff where the soil is good, the rocks warmed by sun, the winds soft, and the land accepting. But only for a time …

Senior Year

After football, things came together.

I first noticed her as she stood in a Sunday school classroom after church. She was an underclassman, but she had a bright prettiness and seemed grown up for her age. A few weeks later, after football season was over, I asked her out to a Saturday night school play.

The play was over around 10:30, and Becky had to be home by eleven—not enough time to drive to any good restaurant in the area. I didn't want to take her straight home, but the only place close by and still open at that hour was the Skylark Restaurant. High school kids didn't hang out there, but at just a half mile west on 224, the timing could work.

We ordered dessert, and the service was slow—we didn't get out until about five minutes to eleven. But Becky lived in a nearby Canfield neighborhood, just across town. Five minutes would be enough time with a minute or two to spare.

As we drove east on 224, ahead at the railroad crossing, lights at the track started to blink red. A moment later, I heard the train whistle blowing from the south—the Erie local was running late, coming back through Canfield on his way north to Niles. I braked as we neared the flashing lights, and off to the right I saw his headlight moving slowly, still a safe distance down the tracks. I knew there wasn't enough time to wait for that train and make it by eleven. "I wouldn't normally do this," I said, "but we need to get you home." I stepped back on the gas, and we thumped over the rails, leaving the train behind.

190

For Christmas, I wanted to give Becky something special. Using a photograph of her, I thought I might be able to draw a simple black and white silhouette of Becky's face, like a sidewalk artist might do. I could place it in a nice frame as a present.

So I tried my hand at capturing her profile. But little had changed since my days of 6th grade art projects. Despite new motivation, I still couldn't draw—not even something as simple as an outline of a person's head. I struggled at the task for over an hour before I finally realized I couldn't do it.

After some thought it dawned on me that maybe I could ask Elizabeth to do it for me. She was one of the best artists in the class—a simple sketch like I wanted would be easy for her. By then I was OK that Elizabeth wouldn't go to the prom with me when we were juniors. And since we had been friends--more or less--over the years, I thought she might be willing to make the drawing. So the next day at school I explained to Elizabeth what I was trying to do and asked for her help. She agreed, and I gave her the photograph.

A couple days later I drove to Elizabeth's in the evening, a big home in town with a wide porch. The porch light flicked on when I knocked, and Elizabeth met me at the front door. She handed me the small silhouette she had created from the photo—it was perfect. "Gee, this is really nice," I said. "I never could have done anything like this. I sure appreciate it. Thanks a lot."

"You're welcome," she said, and smiled politely. It seemed the two of us had come to some sort of understanding. I got back in the car and drove home.

The framed drawing made a nice Christmas gift. I think Becky liked it, although she seemed a little embarrassed to receive a picture of herself. Perhaps it wasn't the perfect gift idea, but she appreciated it, and I believe her father may have liked it more.

Becky and I became a couple, walking together in the hallways during school and talking on the phone at night—the same routine other upperclassmen had followed over the years. Against the odds, somehow I had managed to stumble onto one of those winning Irish Sweepstakes tickets.

The rest of senior year was full—a merry-go-round of activities. There was honor society induction, selling Christmas trees by the fire station to raise money for American Field Service, daily after-school meetings, assemblies to welcome Bonnie back from her exchange student time in Australia and to send Jerry off to study in South Africa, cheering for Richy, Greg and the rest of the team at Canfield basketball games, Saturday night dates with Becky, fun roles in a couple school plays, preparing talks for Mrs. Hall's Speech class, no agonizing at prom time over whom to ask, singing in the choir at church, and morning drives to school with Nancy in our "Blue Bomb," a clunker of a 1960 Corvair that Dad picked up somewhere cheap. And somehow it all felt like winning.

Being a Jerk

In high school, I normally obeyed rules and stayed out of trouble. Some of that probably followed from my 4th grade embarrassments. But there was a second reason, too. When kids broke rules, the things they did—like skipping class—never had much appeal. "Why skip class?" I thought. "You're just going to have to make up the work, and it's only going to be harder if you don't know what's going on." Since the crime had no allure, no upside in the first place, why invite trouble? So I earned a goody-goody reputation at school. But my perspective on following the all rules changed somewhat senior year.

"Mom! Bob's being a jerk!" That's what Carol and Nancy would complain to Mom when I teased them for no reason and didn't know when it was time to stop. "Just Being a Jerk" was the kind of trouble you invited when you got too full of yourself and wanted to have some fun. "Just Being a Jerk" behavior wasn't malicious—it just didn't care.

Mrs. Hendricks taught Civics. She and her family had moved to Canfield from somewhere in the South a few years before. She amused students when she mentioned shopping back home at Piggly Wiggly food stores. None of us had ever heard of Piggly Wiggly—the name invited ridicule, and the ridicule spilled over to Mrs. Hendricks. She didn't deserve it, but kids liked to give her a hard time—probably because we saw our teasing really irritated her.

Greg and I had outgrown Halloween and pea shooters years before. But as I drove to his house the evening of October 31st, beside me on the front seat were two small masks, a couple of sturdy pea shooters, and half a dozen two-pound plastic bags of dried navy beans. Greg lived near the new high school, just a couple blocks from Mrs. Hendricks. The evening was dark with a haze of fog and patchy on-and-off-again drizzle. When I got to Greg's, we put on dark jackets, stuffed bean bags into our pockets and walked off toward Mrs. Hendricks' house. A few young trick-or-treaters were out, prowling in full Halloween costume, so Greg and I blended with other dark shapes moving about the streets.

At the wooded lot next to her house, we ducked away from the street and worked our way quietly into the bushes, taking up position in a thicket of soggy weeds and small trees. There we crouched low, perfectly concealed. From that spot, we had a good view of the front walkway, with a clear shot at the entire front and left side of her two-story house. Lights illuminated windows on both floors, and the porch light glowed for trick-or-treaters. The large home was covered in aluminum siding.

We waited a few minutes for a group of children coming up the front walk—we didn't want to scare them. They rang the doorbell and collected their treats. After the door closed and they left, Greg and I launched the first barrage across the front. We didn't just pop a single bean or two, but took a mouthful of beans and spit them out the pea shooters all at once--ten or fifteen at a clip. Dried beans rattled into the siding like machine guns—the clattering was much better than I had expected! Then we stopped.

193

The living room drapes opened and someone looked out. Another upstairs light came on. Greg and I sat quietly. In a few minutes, the drapes closed. Nothing happened. After another few minutes, we fired another couple broadsides against the far corner of the front. Beans bounced and banged against the metal, and again we lowered our pea shooters. The porch light went off, and then the living room light. All was quiet for a minute, then a skeleton, a devil and Batman came walking up the front steps and rang the doorbell. The porch light came back on, and the door opened slowly. Mrs. Hendricks studied each kid in the group as she handed out candy, looking for clues. When the kids were gone, we waited awhile and then sprayed a couple long volleys against the front and the side, up near the roof line. Then we held our fire again. This time all the lights on the second floor quickly went dark, followed shortly by lights cut off at downstairs windows. And we could feel those eyes searching, just inside the darkened windows, peering out to find us.

· Our cat-and-mouse game stretched through the evening. Greg and I varied our shots across different parts of the house, suggesting the attack was coming from different locations. We fired, then waited, with long lulls between rattling broadsides. We watched for movement inside the darkened windows and paused patiently whenever kids came begging at the front door. As the evening wore on, Mrs. Hendricks looked more irritated, more suspicious each time she answered the door—she knew someone was out to get her, but who? How many? And where were they hiding?

Sometimes Greg and I waited long intervals between attacks—enough quiet for someone inside to think "They finally quit … It's over…," enough time for Mrs. Hendricks to pause, for relief to surface and her to think "… at last, they're gone." Then we waited a bit longer and blasted the siding again with more mouthfuls of beans.

When the flow of trick-or-treaters subsided, we decided to end it. Greg and I could have crawled away from our concealment, without a word, and vanished into the night, leaving Mrs. Hendricks forever to wonder. But heck! What fun would that have been? Instead we put on our little masks so they covered a portion of our faces, hiked to the driveway, walked up to the front porch and rang the doorbell. When Mrs. Hendricks opened the door we met her with a cheery "Trick or Treat!" She studied the two faces as she opened the storm door to offer candy bars. Then her face tightened--she recognized us and instantly knew we were the ones. She didn't say a word, but glared with narrow eyes and pursed lips. "Happy Halloween!" we sang out as we took her candy. In that moment, I imagine the devil himself would have been more welcome on her front step.

We turned and walked away, and Mrs. Hendricks didn't utter a sound. After all we had put her through, I was impressed with her self control—in her place, I doubt I could have held my tongue. We proceeded out the driveway and turned at the street to walk back to Greg's house. As she watched us walk away, Greg and I didn't need much imagination to think of another place Mrs. Hendricks would have loved to tell us to go.

Mr. Graban taught Physics and earned respect as an assistant football coach. He was in his late twenties or early thirties—young enough to remember what it was like being in high school. He treated students almost as if we were adults, and he'd sometimes devote class time to serious conversations with us on topics that were important to guys our age--like girls, football and the new Batman program which aired on TV that fall. But even those credentials weren't enough to shield him from the stupidity of a bunch of seniors "Just Being a Jerk."

There were about fifteen senior guys in Physics class—no girls had signed up for the course. Mr. Graban kept a big wooden paddle up front by his desk. But discipline in his class wasn't an issue—he never needed to use the paddle. Students listened to Mr. Graban and respected him too much to challenge him and force a confrontation. So the paddle merely collected dust--more of a conversation piece than anything else.

One day we were working together in class, and Mr. Graban was at the blackboard analyzing the interaction of gravity and projectiles, diagramming vectors and calculating trajectory formulas. An assistant from the office came to the door and interrupted. "Mr. Graban, could you come to the office for a minute? Mr. Francis wanted to ask you something." So Mr. Graban put down his chalk and instructed us to finish reading the section we'd been discussing and to begin working on the problems at the end of the chapter. Then he exited the room, leaving us alone.

The class stayed quiet for a couple minutes. But then a few of us began talking rather than reading. Gradually, the talking grew louder—we had ignition and lift off. By the five minute mark, the noise was climbing high and laughter mixed in. The "Just Being a Jerk" force was accelerating.

With the seven minute mark, the second stage fired, and Mr. Graban's constraints were jettisoned far behind—no one was quietly reading or working, a couple guys were strolling around the front of the room, goofing off and carrying on, and our noise was spilling into the hallway. We had broken free from gravity, from the pull of caring. So as Mr. Graban returned through the hall and approached the room a few minutes later, the noisy chaos that met him was anything but an ordered Physics class.

He stepped inside the doorway and stopped. He didn't have to say much—his look rattled us back to earth. The noise halted abruptly as guys quieted and returned to their seats. Mr. Graban then walked to the front of the room, to his desk, and stopped. He was thinking. The class had acted up; now he was calculating his reaction.

He leaned over and picked up his paddle, and then he placed it on his desk. Deliberately, he then calmly walked out of the room—we didn't know where he was going, but we had a pretty good idea of what was coming. A couple guys whispered and tried to laugh it off—"We're going to get paddled!" It would be a big joke—a bunch of seniors getting paddled. "Just Being a Jerk" wasn't easily fazed. When Mr. Graban returned to the room, he was followed by Mrs. Lantz, our young Trigonometry teacher whose classroom was nearby. She stopped and stood just inside the doorway. Mr. Graban returned to his desk.

"I've asked Mrs. Lantz to be here for your punishment," Mr. Graban said.

He had made just the right calculation. If we had been left to ourselves, if it had been only a bunch of guys in the room taking turns getting paddled, there might be some hint of discipline or shame about it—but nothing significant. Mr. Graban knew that afterward our big senior egos would joke about it, make light of the punishment and laugh off the whole episode. But with a young woman watching, the paddling would strike something more than our rear ends. It would smack with humiliation.

So one by one, we walked to the front of the room, bent over, and Mr. Graban gave each guy two good whacks. It hurt a little. With Mrs. Lantz looking on, it left a mark.

Later that day when Mrs. Hendricks heard that senior guys in Physics had gotten paddled, I imagine she probably smiled to herself, comforted that sometimes even senior jerks get what they deserve.

Early senior year I knew I had a good thing. I didn't want it to end. So I concocted a plan to stay in Canfield an extra year--a scheme to postpone going off to college. The idea was the antithesis of Carl's old drinking fountain maneuver to reduce class time. But it was creative—even he might have liked it.

I figured that as senior year progressed I could work extra hard and master all the course work, all the learning and academic requirements. But when it came time for the tests, I could purposefully fail the exams—after all, there was no law that required you to <u>try</u> to do well on exams. If I failed all my courses, the school couldn't possibly advance me, and I'd have to repeat senior year. Then, since I would have already learned all the material the first time around, senior year on the second go around would be easy. I wouldn't have to study much, and I'd have more time to enjoy myself.

I knew the scheme wasn't perfect—there was a cowardly element to it, a fear of facing change. But it seemed to have some merit—I was half serious about it. But Becky didn't think much of it, and my parents thought a lot less. I guess I was grabbing at straws, trying to avoid the inevitable.

I knew what had to be done.

It was time to get serious again.

It was time to leave.

Graduation

Canfield offered pat answers to almost any question. What is water? In Miss Burgoyne's Chemistry class we learned water formed when electrons of two hydrogen atoms merged with the electron field of an oxygen atom. Why is Europe divided by an Iron Curtain? Colonel Bennington's history class taught that the Soviet Union built the barrier after World War II to keep their people in and western ideas out. How can two blonde parents have a child with brown hair? Biology texts explained how dominant and recessive genes can combine to produce children with characteristics different from those of their parents. Why are good people killed in car accidents? It's God's will, which mere humans can never understand. Whatever the question, a stock answer was available to put the matter to rest.

Graduates from previous years returned to Canfield from college during holiday breaks and on occasional weekend visits. Many dropped in on high school classes, and some sat in at Sunday school after church. From discussion with them, it was evident many college students returned to town with a newfound disdain for the venerable stock answers. I listened to what they had to say. And while it wasn't clear to me that college kids had discovered new, correct answers to the old questions, some had acquired a different way of looking at things, a view that enabled them to better critique the old pat answers.

So as PSAT's and ACT's culled us out and college catalogues became required reading, I began to look to college as a chance to think about some of the old questions and reconsider some of those stock answers. I didn't expect easy answers in college—for some questions I wasn't sure there were answers at all. But I thought college might open the door to different questions, or different kinds of questions. Questions like … "Why do some groups of people persist in killing each other over the centuries?" or "What's the meaning of the word 'meaning'?" I thought somewhere beyond Canfield such questions might be raised. Somewhere whole communities probably existed where these kinds of questions were discussed, and I began to think it might be possible to gain insight into deeper concepts that truly mattered. The entire world was out there. All that was needed was the will to venture forth.

But when it came time to decide on a college, I chose a small, conservative church school not far from home.

So while we sometimes can look back and remark the path we've come, we can't remake it.

Jerry was class valedictorian. But in January he had chosen to study in South Africa through the AFS program, even though he would miss the end of the school year and graduation. In Jerry's absence, classmates chose me to give the class speech at commencement. It was a serious talk--about the difference an individual can make in the world. Mrs. Hall helped me prepare. My message was sincere, and probably not much more naïve than most other high school commencement addresses. I hoped people might hear something in it they liked. Lemoine was top girl in the class.

One hundred fifty-three Canfield graduates filled the auditorium at the new school, adorned in cap and gown—girls in white, boys in dark blue. Following the presentation of diplomas and the lifting of tassels from one side of our mortarboards to the other, seniors rose a last time, and Pomp and Circumstance marked our ceremony. Then Lemoine led the class down from the stage, through the auditorium isle and into the back hallway. I followed immediately behind her. Our final exit, our going out, was a serious, solemn affair. Not once did Lemoine fiddle with her shoes, I made no attempt to swipe either one, and Mike didn't giggle. The days had wrought their magic.

We proceeded down the corridor toward the cafeteria, where graduates would congregate and family and friends would now gather. I stopped at the top of the steps leading to the cafeteria as the class came by. There passed Mike and Jack, Richy and Jane Ann and Rosemary, Bonnie, Bobby, Greg, Lela, Jeff, Roger and Jim and

Beverly. Graduates were smiles and tearful and proud and happy and sad all at the same time. And on came others—Sally, Larry, Bruce, Kathleen, Paul, Danny and Dave. Elizabeth rounded the corner. As she approached the steps, she turned and landed a quick peck on my cheek and hurried on down the stairway. I turned and glanced after her--maybe she liked my talk? Then a classmate somewhere let out a cheer, and we all shouted and clapped, echoing the joy of the moment. Classmates continued to spill past, and I shook hands and laughed and talked. In a couple minutes, Mom and Dad, Carol and her college boyfriend Steve, Nancy and Becky entered the room. All was celebration.

One last time, there was no place like home.

In geology it's called a stratum--a layer of soil deposited over time upon another layer. Within the stratum, the sediments laid down are formed of the same material and have the same properties. Gradually the elements are compressed to uniformity. In Canfield, we called it a Class.

"Hot as hell, cool as heaven--that's the Class of '67." I think it was Jane Ann who one day came up with the Class Motto. At first hearing, it sounded more like a cheer than a motto. "Be Prepared" or "In God We Trust" were mottos, sayings to live by. "Hot as hell, cool as heaven" sounded like something you'd chant at pep rallies ... then you'd shout "that's the Class of '67!" and you'd expect cheerleaders to spring cartwheels. But whether, strictly speaking, ours was a motto or not, classmates liked the rhyme; it stuck and became official.

Of course, no one in the Class of '67 was forged in the fires of hell or tempered to steely hardness in the cooling waters of heaven— we were just ordinary kids. But something had been at work on us all those years, forming and shaping.

From those earliest days we took in the scent of a fresh loaf of Isaly's Wonder Bread, the smooth chocolate feel on your tongue of a Dairy Isle custard cone, the sweet pink of a water polo watermelon, and the aroma of hot French fries with plenty of

200

vinegar and salt like you could find only at the Canfield Fair. We were formed of the same stuff, the same juices, the same grit.

Day after day, Bonnie and Jimmy stood in line at the water fountain, waiting for Carl to finish. Mike and Richy had fought back jitters at home plate, sweaty hands clutching bat, awaiting that first Little League pitch. Danny and Kathy and Beverly had weathered the thousands of bus rides back and forth from school, shivering February mornings and enjoying cool September air blowing through open windows. Mary and Bobby had come to know the August ritual of checking class lists, morning PA announcements, the rigors of Mr. Wilhide's 7th grade English and the tedium of Mrs. Hall's term papers.

Together we played dodge ball and kick ball and monkey bars, and fought the merry-go-round battles. We shared victories and scrapes on the playground, Cardinal wins on the athletic fields, and the daily accumulation of personal lessons and losses. And each of those days etched its common mark. Until ... like a vein of coal anchored beneath the township, we were pressed with a common core.

Graduation ... the requisite count of seasons had arrived. Another spring had rolled round, and for the Class of '67, our number was up. Graduation--a time for ceremony, a grand gesture, a point to rise up and celebrate all we shared ... and what each had made of it. Graduation ... the last time to move as one ...

Tomorrow the fragmenting would begin.

XI.

Years leave their mark. Time wears the sharp edges of early, fresh terrain. Particles weather, break free and slip downward, smoothing rough edges, filling open crevices, gradually coming to rest within lowlands. Over lifetimes, high sharp ridges soften and valleys smooth. Highs and lows become muted. But within the aging structures, original forms endure.

Reunion

It had been twenty years. Some had stayed, though many left Canfield, scattering to separate lives. I eventually went west, wandered, and met Mel, my sister Nancy's college roommate. In '77 Mel and I married in the Methodist Church on the village green. Ten years later, we were living in the South with our young son. I worked for the railroad.

· When Mel and I walked through the door to the class reunion, I was looking forward to seeing familiar faces and catching up on what had happened to everyone. Mel had come to meet some of the names I had mentioned over the years, willing to listen to others' conversations about old times.

Many friends had returned for the occasion—Jack and Beverly and Nancy, Roger, Mrs. Hall, Danny and Lemoine, Bobby and Richy and Mike and Jane and Jeff…. The years had been kind to most, and it was a rare treat to visit with the past, to sense again a familiar smile, hear a forgotten tone in a voice, and be reminded of a gesture that had long faded from memory.

Mel and I were talking when Elizabeth appeared from the crowd and walked over to say hello. The three of us talked for a minute. She had been living in California, still doing some artwork. Then Elizabeth looked at me and announced with a smile," You know, I had the biggest crush on you in high school." Then she laughed.

Mel and I laughed some, too. But in the same instant I wondered, "Where was I?" I didn't remember that. It didn't make sense. All I remembered was that she wouldn't go to the prom.

But our conversation shifted, the three of us talked a little more, and then Elizabeth excused herself to visit with another classmate. And Mel and I turned and walked over to see Greg.

Later I wondered about Elizabeth's comment. Then I remembered her passing in the hall at graduation, and it started to make sense. "I wonder if she changed her mind about me senior year, when I was with Becky," I thought. That seemed to fit. Then the image of Elizabeth's drawing, the silhouette, came to mind. And the rest of the picture began to fill in.

If my guess was right, asking her to sketch that silhouette probably hurt—but Elizabeth never said a word. "Geez," I thought. "How ignorant could I have been?" I had no idea.

Clearly, Elizabeth had moved on and was doing just fine--turns out that I and my big senior ego weren't such big a deal after all. But Elizabeth's comment and my recollection of the sketch caused me to pause. Faded memories from old Canfield stirred, feelings rekindled, and I was reminded how enduring, how persistent, how tenacious those yesterdays can remain.

Years after, it seemed some things just didn't want to let go. Somewhere within, we're still latched on to that old merry-go-round in the playground, gripping it tight, still trying to yank it along--the boy's way twisting against the girl's way. At some point you'd think the pushing and pulling might have settled down, the momentum would have eased, and over the years the scuffed feelings would have come to a stop. But it didn't seem to work that way. Deep down, it just seemed to keep slowly turning.

XII.

Each today alights our yesterdays, shaping anew tomorrow.

Bedrock

Someday a team of brilliant neurobiologists, doctors and biomedical engineers will develop a new method to peer inside the human body. Theirs will be breakthrough, a revelation, a novel means to scan the brain, sense the heart, and peer into our bones. The complex technique will probe and inspect, calibrate and merge readings, and apply filters, algorithms and myriad computations to translate the data extracted from that host of neurons and muscles and cells into an image of time and place, an image of the experiences first engraved into those tissues.

And if the team were to adjust and tweak the settings on their device to maximum resolution, so they could probe a human's smallest recesses, and the filters and parameters were calibrated and focused just so, gradually from within would emerge the shapes and contours of that individual's personal Canfield—the low hills and gentle ridges covering the township, worn rails spiked down from the north through woods and cornfield, a glimpse of a white-haired man in suit and tie making his way across the green, a forgotten baseball resting in the weeds beyond third base, a dazed stumble in the wake of a head bonk, broad elms shading bright yellow buses emptying from the schoolyard, a swirl of October dust on a dry practice field, the shame of sixty-two to nothing, and strands of pastel crepe paper draped across a gym, sheltering tender dreams.

And deep within that wondrous unveiling, each of those minute cells and nerves yielding its image, each raw fiber of that tissue, will be at work, quivering away, synapses sparking, pulsing, straining to be felt, surging with each experience inscribed against that inner landscape, struggling inside us with the same power and force, the same heat and energy that brings mountains to rise, rivers to flow and the earth to deliver up life.